BK RAJAYOG, TSUNAMIS AND POWER OF SILENCE

DR. D. V. KAUNDINYA MD

[Ex-Professor & Head, Sir J J Hospital, Mumbai

Chairman of MUHS committee to include Ethics and Spiritual Medicine in MBBS course]

BK RAJAYOG, TSUNAMIS AND POWER OF SILENCE

DR. D. V. KAUNDINYA MD

[Ex-Professor & Head, Sir J J Hospital, Mumbai

Chairman of MUHS committee to include Ethics and Spiritual Medicine in MBBS course]

First Published in 2019 by First Step Publishing

Editorial / Sales / Marketing Office at
303-304 Garnet Nirmal Lifestyles Ph 2
Behind Nirmal Lifestyles Mall
LBS Marg Mulund West
Mumbai 400080
E-Mail:- info@firststepcorp.com
www.firststepcorp.com

Copyright © Authors Copyright

All rights reserved. No part of this publication may be reproduced, stored in or introduced into a retrieval system of transmitted in any form or by any means (electronically, mechanically, photocopying, recording or otherwise) without the prior written permission of the author. Any person who does an unauthorized act in relation to this publication may be liable to criminal prosecution and civil claims for damages

ISBN:- 978-93-83306-51-0
Price: India INR 245
Rest $10
Donation to World Renewal Spiritual Trust of Brahma Kumaris, a NGO working for Global Peace, Health and Brotherhood

God's formula for Success

Be Ever Ready, Ever Alert, Ever Attentive, & Ever Active with a high Passion Quotient for

Your Set Goal

1. Watch Peace of Mind Channel 24 x 7
2. Visit the nearest BK Center for a Free of Cost Foundation Course
3. 11500 BK Centers Across 140 Countries
4. Make BK Rajayoga a part of Daily Routine for health happiness and peace
5. Phone : - 09999333555 / 666 for nearest center

Contents

Authors Heartfelt 8

Chapter-1 33

Tsunamis In The Physical World 33

Chapter -2 60

Tsunamis In Consciousness And Wisdom Less States 60

Chapter-3 76

Consciousness And Cosmic Energy 76

Chapter-4 91

Universal Mind, Remote Sensing, Premonition, Remote Viewing, Secret Of Simultaneous Discoveries, Human Mass Excitability Index And Mass Mind Intention 91

Chapter-5 110

Receptorology And Disease Less And Infection Less World 110

APPENDIX – I 119

REFERENCES 142

APPENDIX – II 144

Authors Heartfelt

The main purpose of this book is to make the younger generation realize that ancient Patanjali sutra and Charak Sanhita are evidence based for health and performance enhancement. Dogmatism, divisionism, fanaticism and in the worst **case terrorism** are due to faulty interpretation of the tenets given in different religions. Spiritualism is a common thread that weaves through all the religions. Spiritualism and yogism are necessary for all human beings as the modern fast lifestyle has made the mankind to go against nature and lose the balance in all respects. **Internal balance is lost** giving loss of health, increased pollution and violence. **Global Consciousness Project** has proved that peace in the world could be restored by Mass Mind Intention using prayers and group meditation. **Tsunamis in mind result in the tsunamis of physical world.**

Quick burn out of the young and terrible addictions due to failures in life have become common. Balance between self- merit and expectations from life has been lost. Everybody wishes to own a Mercedes Benz. That is why spiritualism tells us that **all the desires are bad** as they give a restlessness syndrome till they are satisfied. Most funny part is that no sooner a desire is satisfied ,the second one immediately takes its place. **The culprit is the mind** which wants more and more. Patanjali Kriya yoga gives mind control [Mano-nigrah]. **Sleep-wake cycle** has been set against nature. Circadian bio-rhythms or Biological clock inside us has been set in accordance with sunrise and sunset since the origin of mankind. Our nocturnal habits have disturbed it so much that we require to learn "**Sleep hygiene**" merely to get a normal sound sleep. Sedatives become useless after some time. Ancient Vedas are actually scientific formula for leading our lives in accordance with unwritten but actually existing universal cosmic rules. **Laws of karma** are applicable to all human beings. Ignorance about them does not spare you from punishments. The horrific details of the punishment in proportion to Vikarma [Bad karma] are available in **Garud purana**. **Max Muller has said-** "There is no book in the world that is so thrilling, stirring and inspiring as the Upanishads.

German Physicist W. Heisenberg said-"After the conversations about Indian Philosophy, some of the ideas in Quantum Physics that had seemed crazy suddenly made much more sense." Current medical research highlights the value of asana, Pranayama, Dhyana and Dharana in health as well as man-management skills. **Ken Wilber's**

Transpersonal Psychology talks about Atman to Atman transpersonal transactions for effective human resource management and development.

Spiritualism centres around metaphysical God and Atman or soul. Science has not been able to prove their existence. But that does not mean that these entities do not exist. Millions of people believe in their existence. **The definition of GOD** as Governing ,Operating, and Destroying and universally occupying benevolent healing energy becomes immediately acceptable to the **scientist minds**. But the Trinity of Brahma Vishnu and Mahesh immediately becomes labelled as **Indian mythology and myth**. God or Supreme Consciousness is the Supreme Creator, Operator and Destroyer Who creates the material world, provides energy to operate and maintain it and destroys whatever is evil or bad or effete and old. This super-duper scientist is running all the planets in all the galaxies in their pre-ordained orbits with **supreme accuracy** and without any exhaustible material fuel. No scientist till to this date has devised such a machinery. No wonder Sir Albert Einstein was made to say-"**Science is but an infant.**" Microcosm of Dr Deepak Chopra is a part and parcel of vast Universal or Cosmic consciousness. Human Being is a **BMSO- Body Mind Soul Organism**. Body is Humus or soil. It comes from soil and goes to the soil. **Being is**

existence. Being is indestructible, immortal, ageless and disease less soul. **Wellness** comes only when Being is happy. Body consciousness today is so prevalent that the whole focus of drugs and cosmetics is only on the body. **Core personality is forgotten**. Bhagavad Gita tells that all the sufferings in life[Bhog] arise out of body consciousness. Therefore it advises to attain a **soul conscious state of mind**. BK-Rajayoga for me became a practical manual for attaining soul consciousness and thereby get liberation from all the troubles and problems in life. This **exhaustive author's heartfelt** is an attempt to convince the younger generation to include BK-Rajayoga in their daily routine and experience for themselves that they had discovered a **Kalpa vruksha** that fulfils all of their desires -materialistic as well as spiritualistic. **Split second Decisions** give the most accurate solution to the problems or difficult situations. Health comes automatically. Success becomes a foregone conclusion.

Core personality or Atman or sukshma sharir is of prime importance. But we neglect it. One soul several bodies in different births is true. **Past Life Regression Hypnosis and Therapy[PLRH& T]** provides the scientific proof. Body is a costume suitable to our role as an actor in this world drama. **Sanchit karma**[Prarabhda or Karmic Account] decides our costume, our role and the quality of life we have in this birth. Thus the health, happiness, harmony, peace and success in life is **pre-ordained** and occurs as per Divine script which we write with our own hands. BK-Rajayoga gives hope and optimistic solution that your **Bad karmic Load could be burnt out in Yogagni** or fire of yoga and tapasya. Tasting is the proof of pudding. I have experienced it.

Greatest folly a man today commits is that he presumes and assumes the **role of a Doer** while in reality he is just an instrument in the hands of the divinity. In BK-Rajayoga Atman plays the music in tune with divine commandments called as **Shrimat obtained at each Bk-centre through Muralis, a four page script** read in all 11500 BK-centres in 140 countries. Atman in tune with Shrimat performs a spiritual effort[**purusharth**] to attain a Personality of Excellence[**Purushottam**] or more precisely a Brahma type of personality. Charak Sanhita describes 15 types of personalities[prakriti] depending on the level of consciousness. There are three main levels of consciousness- **Satvik, Rajasik and Tamasik. Brahma type** is the highest, purest, most knowledgeful and most powerful among the Satvik personalities. His soul is so powerful that it produces **a beneficial effect on the persons** in contact and purifies the whole atmosphere and nature with powerful and healing thought vibrations. Satanic or Asuri traits in the living beings get transformed into divine traits in a second. **Self-management and man-management** for such a person becomes very easy. He could mould others in accordance with his views. Success in any field becomes his birth right. **Vacha siddhi,** spoken words becoming a reality and **Sankalp siddhi,** the thoughts becoming an immediate reality becomes his usual and natural experience. The paintings of sages doing Tapasya and lions or tigers lolling harmlessly in front of them are not wild imagination but a scientific reality. Ever blissful state[**sat-chit-Anand state**] of consciousness manifests in his personality. Sthit-pragnya state of consciousness or a **state of spiritual equilibrium** becomes evident in such a personality. Grief and pleasure become equal to him in perception. There are eight levels of samadhi[**spiritual evolution**]. A level of 4 or above gives the power to materialize a golden Ganesh idol from thin air. Such super human powers are known as **Siddhis**. At seventh level beyond which eighth level **karmateet avastha** happens, a person comes to know the past, present and future in most precise and lucid terms. This is known as **Turia consciousness** or Trikaal darshee avastha. This is because the microcosm becomes perpetually connected to a cosmic google called cosmic consciousness. Brahma type personality has **two divine qualities [Divya Guna]**- Tejas or glow over the face and Ojas or a soul level attraction for other souls. BK-concepts describe this state as **Roohe gulab** which gives a charisma to the person.

Siddhis even give the power of par-kaya pravesh, kaya-kalpa [rejuvenation to young form], levitation, clairvoyance and astral travel. A book entitled "**Kriya babaji and 18 Yoga siddhas**" by a Canadian, Marshal Govindan and "**Autobiography of a yogi**" by Swamy Yoganand Paramhans describe different siddhas and their miraculous powers. **Maha Avatar Nagraj Babaji** is the first disciple of sixteenth yoga siddha ,Sage Patanjali. One thousand years old Kriya babaji is still existing in the body of a 16 years old young person for the guidance of yogis beyond a certain stage of attainment. Adi Shankaracharya was the first disciple of Kriya Babaji. He wrote a wonderful poem. The gist of the poem told- " Strange was the sight that a 16 years old person, sitting under a Banyan tree and was teaching the aged disciples surrounding him. Still stranger was the fact that the whole transaction was taking place in total silence [without spoken words[**through thought vibrations**]. The discovery of Mirror neurons proves that silent transpersonal human transactions are possible through thought vibrations. The reason for this Atman to Atman attraction or **Ojas** is the presence of mirror neurons in each one of us. The thought vibrations emanating from the soul forms the body aura which could be visualized by Kirlian Body aura photography. BK Dr Chandrashekhar, who recorded a miraculous recovery from a widely spread cancer by **Volcanic Rajayoga Meditation,** made an ingenuous use of Universal Scanner for showing the blocks in Energy Chakras and for recording the span of body aura. **Ojas is a divine quality** [Divya guna] that arises out of the presence of exceptional Right and Left Brain coherence as shown by EEG[Electro Encephalogram]. Such person also has unique and extra ordinary **empathy [samavedana]** for other persons. This Emotional Intelligence or a high EQ[Emotional Quotient] gives an uncanny ability to know by intuition where the other man's shoe is pinching. At the same time such person does try to remove this grief to the best of his ability and give immediate solace to the other person. Such quality creates a natural bonding between the two individuals. The persons then may risk even their lives to save such a philanthropic person. This is the most important quality in **a Leader without title.** The people become his automatic and willing followers. Today in the higher posts of administration, Emotional Intelligence[EQ] is more valued than high Intelligence Quotient. Women have a natural and greater Right -Left brain coherence . No wonder they are the leaders who occupy high positions in almost every organization. Regular practice of BK-Rajayoga confers this increased coherence in men also. Emotional Intelligence is very important in man-management, Human Resource Development[HRD] and in **healthy doctor-patient relationship**. Development of just one divine quality shall reduce the incidence of court cases and assaults on the doctors. But Western medicine lacks a consciousness based approach and so doctors today have become money making machines in a majority of the cases. Greed has been ingrained in doctors as well as Pharma companies.

Magical advances in science and in the field of Artificial Intelligence **[AI]** has conferred miraculous improvement in Working Intelligence**[WI] of the robots**. But the best of scientists in the field of AI have not been able to inculcate Emotional Intelligence in the robots. These brilliant scientists frankly admit that their lack of understanding of the **phenomenon called as Consciousness** is responsible for this vital deficiency. Roger Sperry who got Nobel prize in 1970 for his concept of "One brain and two minds" tells that the Scientist mind in the dominant hemisphere is the root cause of the lack of Emotional Intelligence and most of the problems we face in this world. **This culprit mind** is judgemental about other persons and often finds faults in others. It self-centric and ego-driven. It wants to command and does not know how to mould. It is calculating and its relationships with other persons are based **on self-gains. It** likes to hear its own voice and often has a deaf ear for sound advice. It runs after higher and higher achievements often at the cost of others and its own health. **Winning in Rat race** and cut throat competition against faith and religious and spiritual tenets bring positive outcomes for a short while. But soon they get replaced with stark failures. Their **self-centric** nature[vrutti] creates a negative impact on the workers underneath such persons. **Scientist Mind** is the seat of negativity. It is always full of negative thoughts like lust, anger, Ego, Greed, jealousy, hatred, doubt and repulsion. Today it is filled with stress, anxiety, tension, apprehension, fear worry and frustration out of its failure due to **comparison and competition** with others. Positive thoughts and healing emotions hardly ever arise in such a soul. It requires scientific proof before it can believe and have faith even in the God. Such persons firmly believe that they are self-made men forgetting that with such statements they relieve the Almighty of a terrible responsibility. **Spiritualist Mind** in the other hemisphere functions on belief, faith and positive thoughts and emotions. Philanthropy comes automatically to such persons. Spiritualist mind is the **sleeping giant** lying dormant in all of us. It has immense potential in terms of wisdom, experience and power. The experiences of past several births are stored in this mind. BK Rajayoga silences the internal noise in the Dominant hemisphere or Scientist Mind .This phase has been termed as Internal silence **[Antar mauna]** by the sages. The first and foremost quality this internal silence confers is an extraordinary ability of **Samyak shravana** [Holistic hearing] in which whole of the consciousness is focused on the act of listening. People could remember Veda by merely listening to them once [Ekpathy] because of this extra ordinary ability. The spiritualist Mind is a **super computer**. It tallies the present problem with the data of "Experiences" from the past several births and springs out a **solution almost instantaneously**. This is intuition or gut feeling or inner voice. The uncanny wisdom of going for an **"Extra mile"** comes from this mind. Out of world paintings and innovations come from this mind. Self-determination, self-discipline and self-dedication for achieving a noble goal comes from this mind. This mind also gives a very meaningful **S.W.O.T. analysis**. It makes us realize our hidden potentials and strengths and also the weaknesses. Specific autosuggestions and visualization programme in Bk-Rajayoga removes the weaknesses and potentiate our strengths. Most important is that it confers an ability to differentiate between Opportunity and threat. Many times the threats in life come disguised as wonderful opportunity and the opportunity comes in the form of a threat. A wrong decision at this point of time means great loss or immense gain. Silence of Scientist Mind confers the ability to have an **accurate decision** in such matters. In spite of dominance of Scientist Mind first two seconds of silent transaction between the Mirror Neurons gives the most accurate judgement about the person or an event. This is the weak voice of Spiritualist Mind to help us. But in the **ever present ego** of a person makes him say " Let me think over it." Normally all the thinking is done by the dominant scientist mind. So even after a deliberate delay occurring because of thinking and having **second thoughts**, we take a wrong decision. This is known as **"Harding Error"** that may come in way of snap two second judgements by the Spiritualist Mind.. That is why intuition means listening to your inner voice with more care and attention. Harding error arises out of bodily charms of the other person. Person falls in love at first and then goes on repenting for whole of the life. Harding error is the root cause of divorces within six months of marriage in the younger generation today. Body consciousness brings the error in judgement though an Inner voice has protested.

Self-experience is the best teacher in the world. So here I shall elaborate the importance of BK-Rajayoga practice for health and self enhancement based on **my experiences** in life. I hope and trust that they shall form a **guiding beacon** for younger generation in the present turbulent times. A sharp Saraswat Mind, meritorious educational achievements and self confidence saw me becoming Professor and Head at a very early age of 31 years in Government institution. This was nothing less than a miracle for a Brahmin in reservation oriented system. So my natural conclusion was that I shall retire as the Director of Medical Education and Research. But **God had others plans for me**. So a very apt prayer should always tell God-" Please do not give me **what I desire**. But give me what You plan to give me in life because You know best what is best for me." Bhagavad Gita tells the same thing in different way-" Before time and above the fate no one gets in anything in life."

My posting at Swami Ramanand Teerth Rural Medical College at Taluka place called Ambejogai in the most backward Beed District was the turning point. A **phase of intense problems** began. I was promoted to the post of Professor and Head in 1981. But malignant cast politics of unimaginable intensity made me a victim. An acting and most corrupt Dean of a particular powerful category facing numerous enquiries due to gross financial irregularities, wrote adverse CRs out of jealousy and fear that I may rob his post. He went on taking out his venom for nine years. **This was against rules. Adverse CRs have to be communicated in the same year so that one gets adequate notice** to show improvement. The result in 1992 was that I was demoted to the post of Associate Professor on which I was promoted by MPSC selection **in 1973**. Once again Divinity intervened. A Matt judgement and efforts of **Late Gopinath Mundeji and Pramodji** reversed the reverses immediately so that I remained a Professor with a proverbial Damocles' sword of demotion and transfer hanging over my head. The complete justice was done in **1996 killing all of my chances even to become a Dean**. Thus I missed becoming the Director. BK-concepts and also Bhagavad Gita tell us that "Every moment of the word drama is most accurate and most beneficial. Whatever has happened is good. Whatever that is happening is better and whatever shall that happen in future shall be the best." At that point of time it was difficult for me to swallow this **spiritual wisdom**. My mind kept on asking – **"Why me"?** Retrospectively when I introspect , I realized that every word of wisdom was accurately correct. Had I been promoted as the Director, I would have spent all the remainder of my service kissing the feet of greedy politicians. The **quantum jump in the Quality of Life** I am experiencing after adopting BK-Rajayoga in my daily routine, would never would have come my way. I must narrate some more incidences to prove my point. A transfer from **rural medical college** to advanced tertiary care hospital in **Mumbai** would have devasted many lesser souls. Brain of a Saraswat gave me the fame as examiner who asks tricky and very meaningful questions. At the same time generosity which probably I developed in **the Sangam Yug[Era of confluence]** of previous birth kept me generous with marks. In fact I used to assure each and everybody that your passing marks you have already earned by your mere presence. Answers to questions shall differentiate a distinction holder. **Dr Mrs Kaundinya ,Professor and Head of Physiology, was most popular amongst students as her teaching made** the subject very easy. Students' feedback always told that Microbiology and Physiology are the best departments in teaching. At one of point of time there were as many as **14 distinctions is Microbiology**. In our times Distinctions were rare and exceptionally brilliant person used to get it. So a question arose- Are the students so brilliant or our teaching is out of this world? My mind told me that these two could be contributing factors. **But real performer** is MUHS pattern of examinations with **MCQ, BAQ, SAQ and set of FAQs**[Multiple choice questions, Brief Answer Questions, Short answer questions and Frequently asked questions.] In short it was made very difficult for the student to fail. At the same time setting of the question paper became an **ordeal for the examiners**. Many appointed their juniors privately for such onerous tasks and of course with nothing more than good will which helped in postgraduate examinations. **Dr Dongaokar the first VC** took lifelong and more than adequate revenge over the examiners and medical teachers. The vacations also became reduced to half. **A hell has been created for the medical teachers** and the examiners. Slightest mistake in filling the complicated mark sheets became an offense under **UNFAIR MEANS** and the poor examiner has to report to Nasik at his own expenses like a **hardened criminal reporting to police station where the clerks donned role of a judge**. At MUHS after a wait of several hours revelation used to come that a countersignature was required on a particular page. **Not a single Vice chancellor has made an effort to change the harassing rules for the examiners and a paltry**

sum as remuneration. BK Rajayoga gave such mind empowerment that I did not have to face any such ordeals because of the focus.

Immense stress gave me seven incurable diseases ranging from chronic cough, cervical spondylitis, Thyrotoxicosis, Chronic fatigue, severe back pain due to Spondylolisthesis, tendoachilles tear while practising for veteran tournament and almost a burn out. **Bk-Rajayoga gave impossible and permanent cures.**

Saraswats are God fearing and highly superstitious. BK-Rajayoga gave **emancipation** from several false beliefs and superstition. One of these I must mention. I used to worry on two counts while on the Path of Bhakti.

1] I used to fear that my non-vegetarian food habits surely shall give me a birth in the Yoni of a tiger. Once that happens how I shall hope to become grass eating tiger? Otherwise how I could come back to **human yoni?**

2] Secondly everybody these days is telling that **kayamat or Pralaya** or final deluge is very nearby. How painful it shall be to die by drowning?
Muralis which are from mystical experiences to a human conduit Brahma Baba removed these major

fears. God Himself assured that a human being always takes the birth of a human being. Secondly, India i.e. Bharat never goes under the water as Incorporeal God Shiva always takes Avataran only in Bharat.

Another most assuring part was that God assured repeatedly in His Muralis that He will move with a protective umbrella over your head provided you always remain busy in His remembrance. The **Yogagni** [Fire of Meditation] shall burn out all of your Bad karmic Load and emancipate you from pain and suffering. I have several personal experiences about these novel guarantees by the Supreme Father of all the souls.

The "Experiences" and divine Muralis helped to set an **elevated goal for myself**. Geriatric OPD in Sir J J Hospital revealed to me the End stage battle of the soul before final emancipation as a consequence of unfinished Karmic Load. The visits to old age homes revealed **the hell** that awaits us if we do not shed our bad Karmic load by intense spiritual effort[**Purusharth].**

Interactions with **AYUSH and NCD wing** of Director of Health Services since **2012** revealed the horrible plight of doctors and of everybody in this horrible era called as Iron age[Kali yug] due to stress born NCDs[Non-infectious Chronic Diseases]. **NCDs are non-stop CDs of pain and sufferings**. They include diseases ranging from Obesity, acidity, insomnia , Diabetes, Depression and Heart attacks to cancers, Parkinsonism and Dementia. Suicides, Burn out and addictions are the common consequences. Sometimes the pain and suffering is so intense that there is a cry for **euthanasia or mercy killing.**

Another very serious problem is that noble healthcare profession has become **five star sickness care Industry.** Firstly fall ill and then we shall take care of you at an astronomical cost of course to compensate for our troubles. Falling ill has become a crime for a common man because his illness may devastate the family financially and permanently. No wonder an exodus has begun towards Complimentary Alternative Medicine[**CAM]** which are beyond any control like that by FDA. So several unfortunate people are becoming **victims of quackery**. Modern Medicine promptly declares all such modalities of treatment as " **Pseudoscience" without** making any effort to test the claims of cure by CAMs.

My "experiences" with BK-Rajayoga gave me firm belief that "**An awakening** " of both the doctors and the common man is necessary to make Bk-

Rajayoga as evidence based panacea for all illnesses. BK- Rajayoga is an easy meditation for very busy people today.So Divine Plan made me the chairman of a novel MUHS committee to include **"Ethics and Spiritual Medicine in MBBS syllabus"** in the year 2013.

First problem was the absence of a book that gives consciousness based approach to health and cure- which modern medicine calls as **The Whole Person Medicine**. Supreme Teacher got a book entitled **"Spiritual Medicine for modern lifestyle diseases,"** written by me in the year 2013 itself in mere 21 days while at Bengaluru. This book then went through obstacle race from 2013 to 2018 for getting published. Funny part was that the whole of medical wing of Brahma kumaris felt that my book is not worth publishing by the BK-Literature department. But a **miraculous Divine plan** reached the book to all the International BK-Centres due to **BK Amola Shah of Florida**. Second edition is now getting published by **First Step Publishers in 2019**. A review of the book appeared in Antiseptic Journal in **December 2018.**In the same month, review article entitled – "Meditation versus Relaxation" by myself and Dr Mrs. S. D. Kaundinya got published in the International Journal of Basic and APPLIED Physiology. All of these are miracles in accordance with a Divine script.

Now the next target was to prepare a **short add-on syllabus in spiritual medicine so that MCI permission should not become necessary.** Syllabus submitted in May 2013 became modified to mere **five lectures and five "Experiential sessions"** to be conducted only in the first Academic term of three subjects- **Physiology** at First MBBS level, **Forensic Medicine** at Second MBBS level and **General Medicine** at Final MBBS level. Every care was taken so that the syllabus should not be a burden to the students. Secondly the medical students shall have a prolonged and perpetual exposure for the entire tenure in a medical college of four and half years, to three evidence based mindfulness meditation-

1] Vipassana of Buddhism 2] Preksha Dhyana of Jainism and 3] BK-Rajayoga. The students shall be able to decide which meditation suits them best for their stress management and performance enhancement. Present VC Dr Dileep Mhaisekar had put up the syllabus for discussion in Academic Council in **June 2017. But medically illiterate majority did not allow the VC to implement the recommendations at MUHS level and forced him to submit it to MCI for permission. Today MCI stands dissolved.**

A fresh struggle to implement the syllabus in spiritual Medicine began **in 2019**. The following eminent personalities in the field of medicine have given the foreword for my book-
1] Padma Bhushan **Dr R. D. Lele,** Director of the division of Nuclear medicine, 2]Padmashree **Dr Alaka Deshpande** Professor and Head of Medicine and central Nodal officer for AIDS control 3] **Dr Yusuf Matcheswala** Honorary Professor of Psychiatry at Sir J J Hospital , Mumbai 4] **Dr Naras Bhat**, Professor of Mind Body Medicine , Seybrook University, Sanfrancisco, USA and 5] **Dr Sujal Shah** a renowned Retinal specialist and the President of Jain Doctors" Federation. All of them sent letters to Honourable Academic Council of MUHS recommending the acute need of including Spiritual Medicine in MBBS syllabus. They have pointed out that **USA** has started undergraduate and post graduate courses in Spiritual Medicine in the year 2001 itself soon after **WHO** added spiritual health in its definition of total Health in the year 1998. Other developed countries have followed USA. But India ie Bharat

Is minimum of 18 years behind the world. A great Nation which made the whole world celebrate **International Yoga day on every 21st June** is so much behind in implementing a thoughtful recommendation for bringing a better tomorrow in the present Health scenario, is both **shameful and retrogressive.**

Another very pertinent fact is that the demand for teaching and training in spiritual medicine has been ascertained from the medical students and the specialists by **two CMEs on " Value of spiritual and yogic strategies in modern medicine"** in Sir J J Hospital, Mumbai held in January 2014 and March 2014. Both the KAP study [Knowledge Aptitude and Practice] and Feedback study on two CMEs have been published in medical journal.

A majority [98 per cent] of participants opined as under-
1] They know that spiritual and yogic practices are necessary for their health and stress management. But they are in absolute confusion. There are multiple yoga systems and each one tells it is the best amongst all. Many come in commercial packages. So the mind is unable to decide.
2] They shall never depend upon non-medical self-**proclaimed spiritual Gurus** to learn Yogic practices. They shall always prefer teaching and training by a trained member of teaching Faculty. **Such Faculty which has official recognition could only be created once the spiritual medicine gets incorporated in MBBS syllabus.**

If Dr Mhaisekar succeeds in his ceaseless efforts then MUHS shall be the first Medical University in India which has followed USA and other advanced countries in bringing the syllabus to **global standards**. **NCD wing** shall have adequately trained doctors to apply meditation as therapeutic strategy. Alarming rise of NCDs in young population shall be checked and may be eradicated. Health Budget of Maharashtra could be drastically reduced. My dream of "My India, Healthy, Happy and addiction free India" shall become a reality.

Robin Sharma has given excellent recipe for success in life in his two very wonderful books.. But they become practical and applicable only if person has an empowered mind **and** health by regular practice of BK-Rajayoga. The book "The monk who sold his Ferrari" describes an American advocate who was busy enjoying everything fast in his life. One day he collapses in the court room with massive heart attack. His doctor gave him two alternatives- "Leave the practice to live well or continue with the practice and drop dead eventually." The advocate wanted to go to Himalayas .So he sold his practice to his assistant. The first chapter begins with the assistant burning the midnight oil when a 30 years old person forcefully enters his chamber. The assistant mistook this person to be the son of his former employer. As it turned out the former employer himself was standing before him. I am sure this kaya kalpa[Magical rejuvenation] has happened because of the kriya yoga that sages in Himalaya taught him. Robin Sharma has not elaborated on this aspect. The second book gives magical formulae for success in life by discovering a leader sleeping silently in all of us. But I believe that these formulae shall never succeed in bringing out the desired transformation unless and until help of daily BK-Rajayoga is taken. The much needed self-determination, self -dedication and self- discipline comes only sadhana of BK Rajayoga.

12 March 2019
Dr Dilip V Kaundinya

Chapter-1

Tsunamis In The Physical World

A] Tsunamis in the gross world:-
God, Param Atma Shiv, tells us that this is the end even of the end. The forces of devil are most powerful in the present times which are called as Ghor kali yug in ancient scriptures. The calamities strike all of a sudden. For instance the tsunami when it strikes, all other live beings except the highly evolved human being gets a warning. The other live beings then run away from the scene of calamity and save themselves. But human being has to depend on advance warning systems. Time of India dated 24-12-2018 gave shocking news. A tsunami struck suddenly even when a most advanced system of surveillance was in place. Death toll was 212 or more. Similarly a sudden of the overhead bridge, a sudden cloud burst or mysterious disappearance of a huge aeroplane or the mysteries at Bermuda triangle or a fined tunes aerospace shuttle getting destroyed at the last entry point to the earth indicate that there are certain forces which act unnoticed by science or even human imagination. Here are some points which indicate to an atheist there is a wide scope for believing in God. A group of hard core scientists

whom I was addressing on BK-Rajayoga as Mindfulness meditation for holistic health, told me frankly-"Doctor, please pardon us. All of us do not believe in God." Upon this I asked them "Do you bliee in Energy?" All of them uniformly told "Yes, because energy is everything." Then I told them if I talk about a benevolent universal, all pervasive energy that Governs, Operates and Destroys the effete or evil, would they believe? This cosmic energy, G.O.D. to common masses, is accurately operating the movements of planets in all the galaxies of the Universe for eternal number of years without use of any fuel or without any glitches. Is it not a miracle? Does it not show the existence of a Supreme Creator of limitless intelligence which is well beyond the grasp of most brilliant amongst the scientists?" In short I wish to convey that there are several entities which are beyond the control of a human being. The unexplained sudden destruction must have been designed to restore the balance in Nature by a Supreme Governor, Operator and Destroye [GOD].

B] Tsunamis in human Being [Microcosm]-
A human being is a super duper car manufactured by the Supreme Creator. Latest branch of medicine, Mind Body Medicine calls a human being as BMSO- Body Mind Soul Organism. Unfortunately even today, when the medical science is most

advanced, nothing is known about the mind or the soul. Eminent scientists working on Artificial Intelligence confess that they could improve the Working Intelligence of robots beyond wildest dream. But they shall never be able to incorporate Emotional Intelligence [EQ] or emotions in a robot. Love, empathy, happiness, peace, or hatred, jealousy, stress, frustration or any other toxic emotion could never happen in a robot. Hence in robotic surgery, the performing hand never shakes. But at the same time on the spot improvisations that may become necessary because of a congenital anomaly could never be done by a robotic surgeon. Thus God made machine is simply indispensible.

It would be highly interesting to note that God made BMSO car requires unique maintenance to make it last for 150 years without any disease or infirmity as in Golden Age which has been prescribed in ancient Indian Patanjali Kriya yog. Huge texts are appearing on magical Kriya yog for health, cure and rehabilitation in the recent textbooks of Physiology. Modern medicine showed miracles like heart or kidney or liver transplant. But a brain transplant remains elusive. This deficiency shows that even the intellect is God given. Otherwise everybody could have become a super genius like Einstein by growing Einstein brain cells in the laboratory and having their transplant. Stem cell therapy promises to recreate any lost or damaged tissue in heart, liver, kidney or a knee. But growing into full-fledged brain remains beyond the powers of these totipotent cells. Another striking feature of all these advanced strategies and therapies is success rate is not hundred per cent. Secondly, most important victim of all the modern strategies is the Quality Of Life [QOL]. Expenses devastate the families financially. Glitches always remain. A replaced cataract lens may become suddenly hazy requiring laser treatment. Immuno-suppressive therapy used in transplant or cancer patient gives dangerous side effects and sufferings. Hair loss in a cancer patient after chemotherapy is most traumatic. Stitches after a cancer surgery suddenly come out requiring another operation. Karma theory in ancient Bhagavad Gita explains he reason for these sufferings most logically and precisely. But modern Indian doctors under the delayed Macaulay effect do not have faith in Bhagavad Gita. They require a British or Foreign person to tell them that today Bhagavad Gita is considered as the most powerful book on Psychotherapy. Arjuna was the first case of sordid depression revived by quick-fix psychotherapy given by Lord Krishna on the battlefield.

A host of new diseases have arisen in the recent times which could aptly be named as GOK diseases or God Only Knows diseases. Older infections like malaria, Typhoid and Dengue are appearing in new and most virulent Avatars. Their atypical manifestations are googlies for the clinicians. A battery of advanced but very expensive tests and investigations are spine breaking financially for a common man. Five star medical education and sickness care industry have introduced the element of insatiable greed at the cost of proper patient care. The hospital charges suddenly become more exorbitant once they know that the patient is covered under health insurance. Huge ego of newly rich doctors does not allow time to listen to the complaints of the patients. Simplest cases which were diagnosed merely by a thorough clinical examination previously are sent for MRI and CT scan for diagnosis. The injury is added to the insult when in spite of huge expenditure, the doctor is unable to diagnose the case and therapy consists of shooting arrows blindly in the hope that something may seek the target. Dangerous Adverse Drug Reactions [ADR] are in majority of the cases are iatrogenic or clinician created. My highly revered medical Professor Emeritus of Medicine and Father of nuclear medicine in India, Padmabhushan Dr. Ramachandra Dattatreya Lele wrote an excellent book on "Clinical methods for physical diagnosis. A Chinese took several hundred copies on the day of release of the book. I tried to tell my students at

Sir J J Hospital, Mumbai to purchase this excellent book which shall make them wonderful clinicians like Padmabhushan Dr. Lele and Padmashree Dr. B.J. Subhedar at Nagpur. Today the doctors have forgotten the art of doing percussion. The percussion done by Dr. Subhedar sir used to resound in whole of the ward. The area of dullness of the note used to be precisely clear. Several diseases wee diagnosed by mere examination of the pulse. Thus a correct clinical diagnosis without any expenditure guaranteed a quick cure because of the target specific therapy. This frugal British mode of treatment has been replaced by expensive American Strategies of treatment modalities. No wonder, when a patient dies, the patient's launch an assault on the doctors. A huge American study described in the book "Blink" by Malcolm Gladwell has showed that a doctor who spends only ten minutes of "Quality time" listening to the patient's grievances never faces court cases even if the evidence showed he is guilty. Almost all of the patients and their relatives said-"How I could go to court against such a nice person and the doctor?" In short the tsunami of frustration and hatred in the minds of the patients or their relatives arises because of the callous and emotionless behaviour of the modern Indian doctors. The age old God like image of the doctor disappear. Image of greed stricken, stress stricken, frustration stricken greedy monster who is an easy prey for "Honey trap" and "Money trap" set by th devil is the current image of the doctors. Healing profession has become a sickness care industry. Thus both the healer and the patient approach each other carrying a tsunami of Vikara or toxic emotions for each other.

Omnipresent and omnipotent tsunami of stress in the human beings in every walk of life has given rise to a set of novel diseases which were called as Stress Associated Diseases[SAD].They make the sufferer really sad while doctors enjoy a hay day. Today nomenclature calls them as NCD or Non-Infectious Chronic Diseases. These diseases last a life long and the patient becomes a hen laying golden eggs for the doctor. The fad of "Latest molecule" and "Treatment by browsing Google" not only adds to the woes of the patients but also to those of doctors. So some doctors have made it customary to ask the patient if he is "Google informed" and charge him heavily if he is so. Such patients do not have any belief and faith in the treating doctor. So he usually has a very long list of complex questions. Treating doctor then feels as if he facing a viva-voce in MD examination. In fact having faith and belief are the most essential part of the therapy. Several studies in the Journal of consciousness have appeared in the present times which show that the placebos have become 70 to

300 times more powerful than the drug. These findings have shut down several drug companies in USA. American FDA is very strict. If a placebo is stronger even 30 times more than the drug then it is concluded that the drug is useless. Tsunami of toxic emotions running through the minds of the patients does not allow them to have faith in the doctors. It is believed that belief and faith activate the ultradian rhythms or pranik healing mechanisms described in ancient Indian scriptures. Thus the claims of miraculous cures by different modalities of therapy in CAM or Complementary Alternative Medicine may not be fake. But they need to be systematically evaluated in the Research institutes using state of art equipment that is available now. Proactive Dean of Sir J J Hospital, Mumbai, Padmashree Dr. T.P. Lahane purchased a very expensive chemiluminiscence machine for the Biochemistry department. This machine could finish all the work load of routine investigations in just four hours. In addition , it has a attachment called Verna which directs a tiny portion of one drop of blood for estimation of rejuvenating neurohormones from brain that are released in the blood during a mindfulness meditation like BK-Rajayoga. Stress hormone, Cortisol, is also estimated for effective stress management. But unfortunately no postgraduate student dares to undertake a thesis on the topics in Mind Body

Medicine or Spiritual Medicine. The reason is most practical. The novel subject is not the part of current MBBS syllabus. Any examiner could easily reject the thesis on this count turning the efforts of thee years into a waste. USA has done it for both undergraduate and postgraduate medical syllabi in 2001. This was soon after an Indian initiative and perpetual efforts since 1984 by Dr. Bisht and his associates resulted in WHO adding spiritual health in its definition in 1998.Other advanced countries have followed USA. Thus it is most shameful that Indian medical syllabus is 18 years behind the global standards. In short, tsunami created in the minds of postgraduate students by topic o spiritual medicine has become the greatest hurdle in initiating a thorough research on meditation. My book "Spiritual Medicine for modern lifestyle diseases 2018" reveals that even a standard definition of the technique of meditation is not available. This makes the task of comparing different studies impossible. I have also suggested a composite definition for acceptance in meditation research.

Alarming rise in the incidences of NCDs forced the Directorate of health services, Maharashtra to open an independent NCD wing in 2012. But the doctors today remain ill equipped to tackle the immense challenge because of the want of proper teaching and training in ancient yogic and spiritual strategies and in spiritual medicine or Soul Mind Body Medicine.

High blood pressure, Diabetes, Heart attack, cancer, Depression, Dementia, Alzheimer's disease, Parkinsonism, obesity, arthritis, auto-immune disorders, degenerative diseases like macular degeneration giving blindness, cardiomyopathy, muscular dystrophies, Attention deficiency disease, Idiopathic Bowel Syndrome[IBS] giving intractable diarrhoea and host of several other NCDs write a non-stop CD of pain and sufferings and create a hell for the modern man. An emerging medical science called Receptorology tells that God could easily punish us by alteration in the function of any of these powerful points. For example- genes if modified could give a number of genetic familial and hereditary disorders. The spiritual Knowledge given by the Supreme soul, now known as BK-Gyan tells us that All Merciful God never ever judge us or punish us until our last breath. He, in His unlimited mercies, goes on pardoning our sins and gives divine direction called Shrimat for much needed course correction in our present lifestyle. It is our Sanchit Karma[Accumulated bad karmic Account] that brings misery, pain, heartbreaks, diseases, defects and disabilities in our life. But I have come several souls who in their ego refuse steadfastly to hold the proffered hand of God and continue to suffer in the hell created with their own hands and with their own brand of thinking pattern. That is why BK-Gyan tells us that thought power and our mind could either make you or break you. I have come across several of my doctor friends who suddenly develop a cancer, or undergo a surgery or even worse, a scheduled eye surgery getting postponed because their carefully controlled blood sugar comes suddenly high on the day of operation. They rigidly refuse to accept that tsunami of stress has given the rise of blood sugar and the fault is with their mind.They refuse to understand that religious attendance in the sermons of at ISKCON or diligent religious functions at home or austerities like waterless fasting are not going to bring a change in their mind set [Vrutti], perception and behavioural pattern. Current research in Mind Body Medicine in USA shows beyond doubt that one requires an evidence based mindfulness programme or Meditation to bring about an effective Vrutti nirodh, a prescription for total or holistic health given by the sage Patanjali thousands of years ago. A peculiar mind set effuses to believe in the existence of God and the soul until a scientific evidence is shown to it. Such mental affliction, today, is called as Scientism. The most unfortunate part is that such afflicted person does not even realize that his thinking pattern is bringing the harm only to himself. Self-realization by BK-Gyan and meditation brings about emancipation. I have got rid of seven incurable NCDs by a diligent and regular practice of BK-Rajayoga. This could be called as "Experiential evidence" on which therapies in Ayurveda and Unani Medicine are based. Science may or may not be able to prove that sugar is sweet. But the "Experience" of sweetness one gets after putting the sugar in the mouth clinches the issue within seconds. All of the meditative techniques are based on the "Experience of transcendence or going into a higher plane of consciousness."

Some novel GOKD's- god only knows diseases-

1] GOKD-1- Intractable obesity- Today childhood obesity has risen up to 80 per cent and adult obesity has become a global epidemic. Several commercial and expensive diets have appeared on the scene of market. Each one assures hundred per cent success. Experience and the record of expenses show us what we have really lost. Forty different diets have been described as anti-obesity regimens. But none is successful. Some have given rebound obesity in greater proportion. One Japanese diet claimed to have a "Fat magnet." This is most dangerous. Our sex hormones, Some of the vitamins and our brain are rich with lipids. High protein diets have given kidney damage in long run. Any preserved food material like Maggie is harmful for health. Preserved fruit juices have lost everything that is vital on storage except high sugar content. All colas are carcinogenic. Preservative potassium Benzoate ionizes in the presence of Vitamin C and Benzoate combines with Sodium molecule for which it has higher physical attraction. This is a sort of extra marital relationship. The product Sodium Benzoate is most powerful cancer producing agent. The current fashion of enjoying a sandwich with cola in American style has given a phenomenal 45% rise in the incidence of the cancers. The High energy drinks like Red Bull have dangerous content of caffeine. It transforms a intelligent person into a brain deficient bull within no time. Indians have unique brains and heart. Heart vessels are thinner and they develop multiple blocks. So the number of stents required is always more in number. Chances of rupturing a heart vessel are more as the smallest foreign stent may prove to be bigger in size than he vessel. BK-Rajayoga has given a miracle of CAD-regression, ie the regression of heart vessel disease. But this free of cost celestial remedy is chosen only by very few persons.

The most important factor that gives rise to intractable obesity is the loss of internal balance between the "Hunger centre" and the "Satiety centre" due to omnipresent stress. Leptin is always secreted due to real or imagined stress giving over eating. Ghrelin is produced very late due to oppressed satiety centre. BK-Rajayoga restores the internal balance and gives a miraculous cure of the obesity. Right now, this statement is restricted to an individual "Experience." But a systematic study in modern research Institutes should be able to clinch a correct derivation.

2] GOKD-2- IBS- Idiopathic Bowel Syndrome-
A most commonly used anti-diabetic drug results in this harassing disease during a prolonged use. The bowel moves very forcefully and then the victim has no alternative to but to rush to he nearest lace where he could evacuate. This is the most terrible handicap for a person.

3] GOKD-3-A very wealthy Sardarji lies in an ICU of a famous hospital in Indore as if in deep sleep. All of his systems ae normal as certified by different specialists at the cost of heavy consultation fees of course. They examine him daily for more for making sure that they continue to get their consultation fees than any real hope of witnessing a positive change. Every visit sees a change of drug and more investigations. At last some time later, the frustrated relatives started pestering the clinicians with just one question- "If everything is all right clinically and on investigation, then why the patient is not normal?" Doctors continued to shake their heads sadly suppressing the "Truthful Inner voice" that told them, "God Only Knows".

4] GOKD-4- Kikuchi Fuzimoto Disease-[1970]-

A lady in gym went home and suddenly experienced an intense pain starting at left shoulder and migrating to head and toes in a very atypical fashion. Soon fever developed and the affected left side developed weakness [paresis]. Very powerful analgesic at frequent intervals relieved the agonizing pain. But the chances of developing adverse drug reaction increased wih every passing day. All the state of art and expensive investigations done at two separate Healthcare Institutes in Mumbai came negative. Fortunately this hell lasted only for few days. Another patient an IAS officer was referred from Seoni in Madhya Pradesh [MP] with similar complaints. But the fever lasted for several weeks. Most powerful antibiotics were ineffective. Doses of pain killer continued. All investigations were normal. Fortunately all he symptoms subsided as suddenly as they had come. The perusal of literature showed that this is possibly the self-limiting Kikuchi Fujimoto disease described in 1970.

5] GOKD-5-
Resurgent older foes like Typhoid. Malaria and Dengue are presenting with atypical symptoms and signs. Accuracy of clinical diagnosis lost all of a sudden for a clinician who starts shooting arrows in the dark. If the target is hit, it is good luck for the patient. He is saved from expensive investigations and from guinea pig experiments for efficacy of a new molecule.

Newer emergent infections by hitherto innocuous organisms many of whom enjoy lifelong hospitability of the human host for their nutrition suddenly become more ambitious than what they deserve. They invade the host tissues and bring about terrorist like damage. Most of them have multiple drug resistance because of the constant exposure to newer and newer antibiotics A honey moon between a commensal in intestine and an invader like Typhoid bacillus transfers all of the R-factors to the pathogenic Typhoid bacillus in mere one conjugation. A Brazilian strain of Typhoid emerges giving Dombivali fever in Mumbai. Atypical Tubercle bacilli are inherently resistant to most of the commonly used anti TB drugs. Stress in mind gives a TH-2 immune response instead of TH-1 which restricts the spread of Tubercle bacilli. A Miliary T.B. is the consequence. Interferons get diminished and response to viral vaccines is reduced. Killer Lymphocytes which identify and destroy the invader immediately become sluggish. A cancer cell which forms in each one of us after 10 raised to 17 cell divisions normally gets destroyed immediately is allowed to multiply by the lazy leucocytes and macrophages. An alarming rise of 45 5 in all forms of cancers may be attributed to stress apart from food habits and faulty lifestyle.

Such havoc with the immune system in the body happens because of the tsunami of stress in pons medulla of the brain.

Thus the severity of disease and our destiny both are decided by our thought pattern and mind-set. Positive mind-set brings miraculous cures and a negative thinking pattern I a powerful weapon of self-destruction.

6] GOKD-6- Iatrogenic diseases-

Today, in this Iron Age, even a treating physician could be the cause of diseases inadvertently or by design. The heart of the healer is not healthy. Mind is full of tension with nagging worry of repayment of huge loans. Huge capitation fee in private medical colleges gives degree even to the most unworthy. Whole system of education has become corrupt. The Devil traps the weak in "Honey trap" and "Money trap." Ignorance about current drugs makes the prescription of antibiotics for diarrhoea instead of probiotics which use harmless organisms to kill the harmful ones. Antibiotic Associated Diarrhoea could be quit troublesome with super infection by fungi.

7] GOKD-7-Social diseases of unimaginable intensity and profound bystander damage-
All sorts of crimes, violence, rapes and addictions come in this category. Violent tsunami of lust in mind gives rise to "Nirbhaya case." Mindless murder of school going children and Road rage are due to mental tsunami of anger. Scam after scams in crores is due to tsunami of insatiable greed in mind. Money only corrupts but the power corrupts absolutely. Terrorism all over world is a tsunami in mind created by erroneous beliefs and misguidance. Addictions of all sorts are just to get a "Mental kick." Unfortunately the rich and powerful god by a malignant desire to try everything that is new are the unfortunate victims. The abnormal craze or tsunami for variety gave rise to the deadly disease called AIDS.

8] INSOMNIA- SLEEPLESSNESS-
This is one of the commonest NCD which is often misinterpreted. Several people function under a misunderstanding that normal 6-8 hours of sleep is not their requirement. A research has shown that an agile mind more agile than a monkey bitten by thousand scorpions is the root cause of

sleeplessness. Such fickleness of mind does not allow a person to focus for a long time on any matter. The children today are super intelligent. So much so that the geniuses by older IQ scales come in lowest five by modern IQ standards. Nearly 18500 genes have undergone mutation. This event probably heralds the emergence of a superior race of Golden age with Kanchan kaya [Golden people]. But in the present Iron age, the hyper intelligent children have developed ADHD- Attention Deficiency Hyperactive Disease. Many of these unfortunate children grow as adults who change their jobs at the drop of the hat. Eventually their bad reputation makes it impossible to get a job. Usual end is a Burn out, suicide or drug addiction. Research shows that Pineal gland, the seat of the soul, invariably shows calcification in persons with insomnia. One this happens it indicates that the death of the person is very near. Fluoride dental pastes and EMR-Electromagnetic radiations especially from mobile over use are the culprits. Plenty of water intake, green leafy vegetables and Satvik vegetarian diet reverses pineal calcification and also prevents it. The transcendental state of consciousness achieved by regular practice of BK-Rajayoga gives the benefits of deep sleep.

9] GOKD-9

Depression is most common NCD today. The person develops anhedonia [smashaan vairagya] and starts shunning the very activity he liked most. H withdraws himself from social circles and becomes an introvert. The near and dear ones think wrongly that the person wants to remain in his personal space, term that is a common parlance in western world. One has to take person's permission on phone prior to visiting him or prior to sending him an email. The ego driven American psychology makes a person to quit what's app group of close friends when somebody does not bow its wishes and directives. No wonder Depression is very common in Western world. Personal letting out of toxic emotions by phoning a friend is not available. The scenario reminds us that the events in the epic Mahabharata are happening even today. India was under the most virulent and corrupt **Dusshasan** [Bad governance] before 2014.Good governance brought tremendous international prestige to India. It became a matter of pride to tell that I am an Indian. The year 2019 reveals that the mythological story of **Samudra manthan** may be quite real. All the **asuras** have become united to taste the nectar of power one again. Now the fate of India and of divine straight forward people following the **straight path or Sirat al mustaqim** depends on the Right choice. **Duryodhan** [the Devil]is very powerful with all kinds money power and other powers available to him. Unfortunately Bhishmacharya, Dronacharya, Krupaharya and Karnn are in the battle on the side Duryodhan. Kauravas [Adharm, Asuras or Devilish mind-set] are in overwhelming proportion [18 Aukshahani sena] and badly outnumber Pandavas [Dharma or Divine persons]. Even the army of Yadavas [Lord Krishna's army] is on the side of Adharm. **Only The One and The Only One All Merciful** is on the side of Dharma and good governance and He shall make all the difference.

10] GOKD-10-CHRONIC FATIGUE SYNDROME [CFS]-
Chronic Fatigue Syndrome [CFS] has become very common in advanced countries. Person goes to sleep in the place of work in spite of sleeping adequately in the previous night. Several viruses have been discovered in association with CFS. But aetiological role has not been decided till to this date. All the investigations are normal. Cure depends on burning out the bad karmic account by volcanic BK-Rajayoga meditation. Experimental data about the cure by BK-Rajayoga is not available. One has to depend on "Experiential evidence."

11] GOKD-11- CANCERS-

Each one of us develops a cancer cell after 10 raised to 17 cell divisions. But only few unfortunates develop cancers of varying degrees of malignancy and invasion into various tissues as metastases. Natural Killer cells and amazing protective immune mechanisms are present in each one of us. Then why someone just develops a benign growth and is well after its removal and why another person may be his friend or close relative develops a most invasive form of cancer suddenly without any warning? Quest for the answer to this riddle continues. Free radicals attacking nuclei give either cancer or an auto-immune disorder. The attack on cell membranes gives rise to Diabetes or Thyrotoxicosis. Free radicals attack in some gives rise to incurable ILD – Interstitial Lung Diseases forcing the individual to carry a burden of oxygen cylinder for the remainder of his life like the actor Mehmood. Modern medicine is unable to provide a satisfactory and logical explanation to the variation in the fate and destiny seen different individuals. **Karma theory** of two alternatives in ancient Bhagavad Gita provides the answer. Free radicals attack the Longevity genes and reduce the life span. But we also have among us the exceptional persons, especially the **Jain Munis**, who survive a healthy life of 100 to 125 years. Mere genes, fasting, lifestyle and vegetarian diet could not have been responsible for this miracle.

Pain relief today has several modalities as the pain is something which reminds an individual of hell and God. But there is one story of Ramanna Maharshi in South who underwent a surgical procedure without anaesthetic. Meditators who regularly practice Mindfulness programme seem to be bearing the excruciating pain in terminal cancer without much discomfort. Advanced medicine has no answer or explanation.

ANCIENT KARMA THEORY IS REAL-

Today, everywhere we have pain and sufferings around us. A new born who has not yet committed any karma suffers from congenital anomalies and undergoes a series of painful operations. The reason for his is accumulated karma **[Sanchit karma]** of last birth. A well-known sinner continues to enjoy power and wealth when a pious God-fearing person undergoes sufferings of different kind. The man cries and asks God," Why me?" Answer is simple. All apparently good persons in this life were not good at all. Their pain and suffering **[Bhog]** is because of the unfinished karmic account which has not been settled in the fullest in previous birth.

Bhog due to unfinished karmic account is of four types- Of body [Tana], of mind [Mana], of people

[Jana] and Wealth[Dhana]. BK- spiritual concepts as derived from the mystical experiences given to a human conduit by Supreme Soul tell us that Karmic account always gets settled to the last penny [Hisab chuktu hona].This is the last birth for all of us. So karmic account suddenly comes up in the form of diseases of the mind or body, a stranger suddenly comes forth and starts berating you for no apparent reason, a sudden financial loss strikes you like bolt from the blue, a sudden accident robs you of all the fun and pleasure you are having or one may have thoughts and lust related dreams at an age when you are in Vaanprasthashram. The global #Me too epidemic is the proof.

A theory tells that at the present point of time cycle we are surrounded by satanic entities or the souls with unfinished desires. If the mind is weak, these satanic entities take hold of the poor person and use him to satisfy their unfinished desires. A person with Divya chakshu [Spiritual eye] could see them with naked eyes. A book on sir Arabindo by Mr. Dalal describes that our bodies are surrounded by an energy aura which has two types of channels- those for Satanic or devilish entities and those which allow entry of divine deity-like entities that surround us. When we in constant remembrance of the Supreme [Nirantar Dhyan], the channels for only divine entities are open. On the other hand when the mind is full of **Vikalpa, Vikara, Vasana and Vikshepa** [Negative thoughts and toxic emotions] the channels for satanic entities are patent. These devilish entities could then enter our consciousness and take hold of our psyche. Such "Possessed souls" shall then commit the most heinous crimes. BK-spiritualism tells us and teaches us to remain in constant remembrance as a safeguard against the attacks of Maya, Ravana, Devil or Shaitan in our mind. Thus human mind is capable of becoming a wonderful instrument for healing and impossible cures. Or, it could become the most potent weapon for self-destruction.

At every moment of our lives God sends a person or event which is actually a test to determine our **choice- Right or wrong**. Amrut-vela BK-meditation makes us aware about two unique powers residing within all of us-

1]Catching power or touching power [**Self-realization or Mehassosata**]and 2] the power for self-transformation, our older beliefs, faith and superstition under divine guidance[Shrimat] received from celestial Muralis[Sanskar aur swabhav parivartan]. Thus self-realization is the first step to God-realization.

A Secret Global organization called Illuminati-

The origin and existence of this very powerful global organization is probably the best example of the truth in Karma theory. Several hundred years ago Galileo and his associates tried to show to the world that the earth is round and not flat as all of the ancient philosophies believed. Some ruthless religious fanatics murdered Galileo and his associates for their sin in telling something against their fir beliefs. Illuminati took existence to take revenge of the ruthless murders committed in the past. This secret organization has powerful and extremely wealthy persons as members in all the parts of the globe. This organization suppresses any information that is connected with God, religion and healing. They either purchase the person or eliminate him. The book entitled "**Source Field investigations**, Mayan prophecy, ancient civilizations and 2012 deluge" by **David Wilcock**; a renowned scientist gives wonderful and lucid details. Several Russian scientists working on cosmic healing energy around the pyramids disappeared miraculously. Several were sent to concentration camps to die there. **Kozirev** was the only soul who survived and produced a voluminous amount of magical research on DNA energy duplicate of the body and several mysterious phenomena.

Mysterious Pyramid energy could save millions in energy bills. It could preserve fruits, vegetable and meat in original freshness for indefinite period. It could sharpen the old razor blades and make them last for a very long time; it could revive the moribund neonates who were sure to die to a magical health. The oil from the rigs became very pure. The persons in the radius of pyramid energy were healthy and happy. Famines, floods, draught and other natural calamities never occurred in the zone of pyramid energy. The yield from crop was miraculously high. But a **tsunami of pathological greed** in human consciousness saw to it that this magnificent research was thoroughly suppressed.

Chapter -2

Tsunamis In Consciousness And Wisdom Less States

The term consciousness which means an Energy having awareness [Chaitanya Shakti] was well known to ancient Indian sages. Unfortunately it remains an enigma to the western world. Even the great names in the field of Artificial Intelligence [AI] confess that they hardly knew anything about the consciousness. Hence they could improve Working Intelligence in their robots. But incorporating Emotional Intelligence [EQ] in robotics remains an elusive prospect for them. The modern Medicine which is an infant with a history of mere 400 years has a total focus on body. All of the therapeutic strategies address only the body [Humus or soil or Sthool sharir]. That is why **Hippocrates,** Father of modern medicine lamented so many years ago- "Of the greatest error today is that physicians do not take soul [sukshma sharir] into account for therapy." Modern medicine is continuing to the repeat the same mistake even today. No wonder a terrible group of diseases called as NCDs- Non-infectious Chronic Diseases are creating the hell for the patients. The unfortunate victim undergoes all possible sufferings described in horrifying details in **Garuda Purana**. The pain sometimes is so intense that it has created a global demand for legalizing **euthanasia**. It is not small wonder that in spite of witnessing such sufferings even doctors do not have faith and belief in Indian scriptures, and in yogic approach o therapy. The current and standard textbooks of Physiology like that of Bijalani and Best and Taylor have exhaustive chapters on Patanjali Kriya yog and in its importance for health, cure and rehabilitation. Advances USA has more than 70 institutes of Mind Body Medicine since the first one was founded by Dr. Herbert Benson in 1970. Consciousness based approach in ancient Charak sanhita gives the current fashion of Whole Peron Medicine and Wellness in USA. But Indian doctors even in USA remain largely unmoved by profound ancient Indian wisdom in the art and science of healing through yogic approach. Uniformly this free of cost approach to health and cure immediately receives a label of **"Pseudoscience"** from modern mainstream medicine without any effort to investigate the claims of magical cure on scientific anvil. There is no realization that this very Vikarma of modern medicine is making **quackery** a thriving business. Even the sex robots cannot give **trupti** [Total satisfaction] only because of the lack of Emotional Intelligence. Bhrushta mati [corrupted wisdom] makes a man like artificial than the real. No wonder pornography on net is the favourite pastime. LGBT is the limited and abnormal quest for new openings. Internet addiction is the latest in the list of self-killing addictions.

Bhagavad Gita gives most logical and scientific explanation for the **genesis of addictions and bad habits**. A thought forms the seed of our karma. A repeated bad thought results in Vikarma under appropriate circumstances. The famous "Inner voice" shouts the loudest to prevent the sin from happening. But modern man with power and money and loss of conscience throttles this voice mercilessly and commits the bad act. Over a period of time with continual bad acts, the inner voice becomes feebler and feebler. A time comes when the man demands instant gratification. Recently arrived ATC- **Any Time Condom machines** cater to the needs of such feeble and corrupt minds.

A bad act when repeated often results in habit or addiction. A HABIT is difficult to cure. Remove H, abit remains. Remove A, bit remains. Remove B, it remains. Then what is the remedy? Remove I or Ego for allowing the fresh input to happen which could bring **self-transformation**. Regular practice of BK-Rajayoga reduces the Ego or Aham appreciably within three month. This derivation is based on **"Experiential evidence"** gain from personal "Experimentation". The **"Inner silence"** of devil or negativity allows **Samyak Shravan, a process in which the whole of the inner consciousness is focussed on the act of hearing.** Ekpathy or Dwipathy, who could recite Vedas after hearing for once or twice, had this unique power of focus [**Ekagra chitta avastha of the consciousness**]. WHAT IS SOUL OR ATMAN?

Bhagavad Gita gives a lucid definition. But the total clarification came to me after a free of cost Foundation course in the BK-centre situated in the Peace Park and Meditation Hut in the world famous **Sir J J Hospital, Mumbai**. Soul or Atman is a metaphysical conscient point of light situated in the centre of the forehead in between the two eyebrows. Tiny pineal gland situated in the brain in the same axis is believed to be the seat of soul by medical scientists. Hence this gland is known as God's spot. It is also known as God's antenna as it is believed that the "Messengers of God "received cosmic messages through this antenna.
Consciousness is a unique Energy which has awareness and it manifests in the Atman in three ways- 1] Mana [Mind], 2] Buddhi [intellect and wisdom] and 3] Sanskaras [Traits].

WHAT IS MIND?

Mind is a virtual screen formed by consciousness on which the thoughts, emotions and desires are formed as transient images. Thoughts and emotions may be good or bad. But the desires are always bad. This is because desire has one powerful propensity. Next desire forms no sooner the first one is satisfied. This gives rise o famous "**Quick Quick syn**drome" or "Hurry syndrome."
Roger Sperry, is a Physiologist who got Nobel Prize for his concept of "One brain and two minds" in 1970. Scientist mind resides in dominant left hemisphere of the brain in the right handed persons. The Spiritualist Mind in other hemisphere is the microcosm or the entrapped divine consciousness. Scientist mind is logical, judgemental, mathematical and always calculating in terms of self-benefits. It is literally a **Devil's workshop** .It is the seat of Vikalpa, Vikara, Vasana and Vikshepa. This is the real devil in our minds. Spiritualist Mind is most powerful and has immense potential in terms of memory, wisdom and experience. It is a super computer which could give an instant and most effective solution to the most difficult problem. This is because it tallies the current data against the innumerable files of past experience and judgement. So h two seconds snap judgements often called as intuition or gut feeling

always turn out to be most accurate. **Mirror neurons** in our frontal brain play a great role. Thus decision making becomes quick and accurate. This unique propensity is greatly desired at higher levels of hierarchy in any type of management and resource development. Spiritualist Mind is responsible for Emotional Intelligence and empathy. The boss immediately recognizes where the other man's shoe is pinching. The most powerful Primary Motivational Factor [PMF] in a human being is love. Spiritualist Mind functions on love, belief and faith. Hope, happiness, energy and enthusiasm all become powerful when the spiritualist mind takes charge of running the affairs of the body. Everything becomes easy, automatic and instantaneous.

INTELLECT AND WISDOM

These two terms are different. Intellect means the ability to learn the skills for earning livelihood quickly. Wisdom means an ability to use the God given intellect properly. Here properly means in accordance to the eternally operating universal laws about right conduct and behaviour. Preservation of Honesty and integrity under any pressure or enticement is the right conduct. It requires a clear and unadulterated consciousness. But it is missing in today's world. Dr. N.N. Wig,

Professor emeritus of Psychiatry at PGI, Chandigarh, tells that a "Spiritual vacuum" is responsible for the loss of power of differentiation between right and wrong. An honest person has peaceful sleep. But a person on Devil's path has tsunamis of negative thoughts in his consciousness robbing the person of the much needed sleep.

HABITS, NATURE [RUTTI], TRAITS, PERCEPTION AND BEHAVIORAL PATTERN

Thought forms the seed of karma and destiny. Bad thoughts [Vikalpa and Vikara] are the most potent weapons for self-destruction. They create a tsunami in Pons medulla giving rise to hell in life by the development of one or more NCDs like Diabetes and high Blood pressure. Every third Indian suffers from this twin epidemic. Repeated bad thoughts give bad habits and addictions. Habit once hardened becomes Nature [Vrutti or Mindset]. Hardened nature is transferred to next birth as Traits [Sanskaras].Nature indicates formation of indelible ridges on elusive consciousness. Traits indicate that s spiritual genome has been formed in consciousness that has the propensity of going into next birth along with the soul or Atman. Several Familial and Genetic diseases are crated in this fashion. So the concept of one soul and several bodies is quite real and scientific. Past Life Regression Hypnosis and Therapy **[PLRH&T]**

proves that the traits and karmic account are transferred to next birth along with the soul.

POWER OF SILENCE

WHY HUMAN BEINGS ARE NOT FOREWARNED ABOUT ONCOMING TSUNAMI?

A continuous tsunami of negativity in Scientist Mind does not allow us to receive the forewarnings which even animals are able catch and act. Inner silence **[Antar mauna]** of negativity in Mind brings about clairvoyance [Trikaal-darshi avastha, Turia state of consciousness]. Sage Patanjali tells that **Samadhi** does not mean that the atman has become one with God by merging in Him. Logically if this could happen, a time shall certainly when all of the souls on earth have undergone merger. If this happens, then there would not be anybody existing on planet earth. That would mean an end of the world. So the BK-concept as told by incorporeal Supreme Creator appear to be most logical. A soul undergoes repeated cycles of birth and death eternally through a time cycle of 5000 years. A human soul always acquires a human body in each birth. So the concept of 84 million yonis before human birth is absolutely irrational. Karma theory shall be thrown into four winds. God shall find it very difficult to tally the karma of a vegetarian human being with that of birth as a carnivorous tiger. Gene theory shall become redundant. Only a human being has been endowed with the power of differentiation between Right karma and wrong karma. If kali-yug or Iron Age continues for millions of years, then merely the huge weight of accumulated karmic account would have flattened a human being as squashed insect on planet earth.

The term **Muni means silent meditators**. BK-Rajayoga is the meditation done in silence for achieving the powerful internal silence [Antar mauna]. Samadhi means conquest over ageing, diseases, pain and sufferings. It involves 8 levels of consciousness. Each level of spiritual evolution to higher consciousness gives an "Experience" of siddhis [Super human powers. First two levels give emancipation from bodily pain and sufferings. Third or fourth level possibly gives superhuman powers [Siddhis] like Sankalpa siddhi and vacha siddhi. **Levitation** or walking over fire and water may be at initial higher levels. Maharshi Mahesh Yogi had performed such miracles in USA. So his TM- **Transcendental Meditation** became quite popular. Sadhak may acquire Clairvoyance [Turia state of consciousness, Trikal –darshi avastha] somewhere between 6th to 7th levels He may also get a siddhi of astral travel. Eighth level is probably the final **Karmateet avastha** in BK-concepts when the soul has attained the maximum level of purity and power. At this point of time the pure soul just cannot reside in the body conduit formed through Vikara. This wonderful spiritual journey of thousand miles begins with your single step. It is my personal experience that once you begin the journey the Supreme Father of all the souls, Supreme Teacher and Supreme Sadgatidata Param-Atma [Supreme soul]helps you by thousand steps. The spiritual evolution and enlightenment then happens easily, quickly and automatically. No wonder that BK-Rajayoga is called as **Sahaj Yog. But the Iron Age** ALWAYS PROVIDES MULTIPLE ALTERNATIVES CREATING CONFUSION IN MIND. That is why one finds several variations of God given Sahaj Rajayoga. There are several spiritual Gurus giving Gyan for a cost of course. There are several religions and their multiple sects. Each one is founded by a Spiritual Guru for self-gains. Mentally confused then seek solace from such greed oriented Spiritual Gurus of Iron age and remain ignorant misguided about the ultimate truth and the real spiritual knowledge for whole of their lives.

Spiritualism opens the mind at **Supraconscious level**. Such sharp mind listens to or reads carefully about different spiritual paths. Analyses each input on the anvil of intellect. Then if the concept is not harmful in any way, it is put to experimentation to derive "Experience from each concept." Experience is the best teacher and inner spiritual mind tells one what is right and what should be discarded. Supreme Teacher then asks us to share one's "Experiences" with others to make them "Experienced." Perpetual spiritual evolution and enlightenment then happens which is experienced in the form of **Chadhati kala**, a rising graph. Regularly attending **Murali** at a BK-Centre ensures perpetual guidance from a Supreme Teacher. One feels as if the Supreme Father of all the souls is holding my hand and guiding me through life on a wonderful journey of spiritual evolution. Each attendance at the BK-Centre provides a unique feeling- "The God Whom the whole world is searching is coming daily to guide me in my spiritual quest.

Shiv Param Atma also tells in His celestial Muralis that intense fasting and austerities, intense Tapasya in Himalaya or becoming Sanyasi by leaving your wife and children to their fate can never ever give God-realization. BK-concept calls this as "**Nivrutti marg.**" Supreme Teacher teaches us **Pravrutti marg**. This means one has to be like Mahaveer Arjuna. One has **to face** his individual inner enemies [Vikara], a difficult person and a difficult situation, fight it and finish it permanently **[Sadaa ke liye]. God, the Supreme Teacher goes on** sending the same type of person or event in your life till you have learnt an indelible lesson from it. The challenges [Vighna] in life become an examination to prepare one for the final split second examination before the soul leaves the mortal coil. It is the Godly training for achieving the glorious titles of master Vighna vinashak and master sarva Shaktiman. A TIME COMES when Maya, Ravana, Devil or Shaitan packs his gloves and bids you good bye in total reverence.

CERTAIN WISDOMLESS STATES OF CONSCIOUSNESS

Greatest enemy of the mankind today is Ego which also means Erasing God Out Of your Life. As a Brahma Kumar I have an experience of 21 years and of 24 different BK-centres. As a part of Medical wing of BK- R.E.R.F.[Rajayoga Education and Research Foundation] I had the privilege of interacting with all-time greats like BK- Dr. Girish Patel, a psychotherapist, BK Dr. Masand [Intervention Radiologist, BK Dr. Shubhada Neel [In charge of SIG for Divine Garbh Sanskar BK Dr. Ashok Mehta, BK Dr. Mirdha, Medical superintendent of Global Hospital, Mount Abu, BK Dr. Avadesh Sharma, Delhi based renowned Psychiatrist, BK Dr. Banarasibhaiji, Director of Medical wing of Brahma Kumaris and BK Dr.

Sachin Parab. Dr. Mehta is the Medical Director of Global Hospital, Andheri, Mumbai and he is a renowned cancer surgeon. He is in-charge of Special Interest Group [SIG] cancer and **VIHASA-Values In Healthcare – A Spiritual Approach.** All of these great Munis and Mahavirs and several in-charge Shiva shaktis may have conquered powerful Vikara called lust. But unfortunately ego manifests in these souls without realizing that it exists in microform [Sukshma swaroop].Micro form of ego makes them perceive that they could never err. The error always is with the other soul. Shiv Baba calls this as Robb which prevents them from having a very **essential realization [Mehassosata]** that every other person is also working to the best of his abilities abilities for achieving the goal of global welfare **[Vishwa Kalyan] set by Shiv Param-Atma.** All of them observe deep silence if an attempt is made to get their valuable advice and guidance on phone, email or SMS. Non-responsive state appears to for whole of the remainder of our lives. This I think is the greatest example of wisdom less state in the present times when Shiv Param-Atma is telling passionately to burn out all of satanic Sanskaras and to celebrate a Sanskar Milan Samaroh [Merging of and solution to all conflicts due to difference in traits]. Shiv Param-Atma also tells that –"Naraz wohi hota hai jo drama ka raaz nahi janata- A person who has not learnt the lesson of "Nothing new" from the experiences in this time cycle continues to harbour ill-feeling and anger against other soul." **The microfilm of EGO is so tough** that even the words of God could not penetrate inside.

SYNDROMES ASSOCIATED WITH EGO

1] **Stiff collar syndrome**
2] **Swollen head syndrome**
3] **Dhrutrashtra Gandhari syndrome**
4] **Abhimanyu syndrome**
5] **High Achiever syndrome** - The person goes on setting higher and tougher goals for achievement one after another. He becomes so busy on this self-centric and self-satisfying **"Hedonic Treadmill"** that he neglects his family and health. He completely loses **work-life balance**. Eventually his karma and destiny brings him to a point of no return. His family members start shunning him and his his health becomes fragile because of constantly going against nature. He realizes the futility of all at the end like Alexander the Great.

6] **Scientism-** Such mind-set refuses to believe in God simply because **infant science** has not yet found a method to prove the existence of God and soul. **Ego** of his God given extra ordinary intellect makes him tell that he shall be able to believe in God, soul and mind when the research on

Neutrino gets completed in NOL- Neutrino Observatory Laboratory in Bengaluru **in 2050.** This statement coming from a ninety years old renowned personality shocked me because of the stark **absence of wisdom** in harbouring such a hope.

The first two syndromes are typical. The person lives enclosed in his own cocoon or Ivory tower wisdomlessly.

Dhrutrashtra type is a genetic anomaly which continues to be wisdom less lifelong. **Gandhari type** purposefully shuts its eyes to reality and wisdom. **Abhimanyu** is a personality type which rigidly refuses to hold the proffered hand of God and continues to drown in the sea of misery, pain and Suffering moving in circle in the vicious and deadly Chakra-view.

Ego in any form or proportion forms the greatest barrier between the two individuals. Ego driven personality loses a very important power of **Samyak Shravan** [Art of Attentive listening] to what other is trying to tell. He loves to listen to only his voice. So fresh input for appropriate, beneficial and effective analysis stops coming to him. This stagnation overtime leads to the loss of team work. The unfortunate person fails to realize that TEAM means Together Each Achieves More.

Hence Ken Wilber, the renowned Transpersonal Psychology talks about **Atman to Atman** transpersonal human transactions for effective man management. Today USA has a huge Ken Wilber's Institute of Transpersonal Psychology. BK-Rajayoga teaches us and trains us thoroughly in having an Atman to Atman transaction with each and everybody for all time [Sadaa **ke liye].**

Chapter-3

Consciousness And Cosmic Energy

TYPES OF CONSCIOUSNESS

1] Macrocosm, Universal consciousness or Supreme Consciousness- limitless, ageless, timeless and vast beyond human imagination

2] Microcosm, Consciousness limited to the boundaries of mind and body. It resides in Spiritualist Mind. This inner giant could be awakened to its full potential only by silencing the dominant Scientist Mind by a mindfulness meditative process. **Mindfulness** means such power over **agile Scientist mind** that it could be silenced in a fraction of a second and could be made to stabilize on a single thought in a laser beam fashion for any length of time. This is the basic principle on which BK **volcanic meditation burns out the Bad Karmic account** and brings about miraculous cure even of the incurable cancer. **EcaP or Exceptional Cancer Patients** in Bernie Seagal series and BK Dr. Chandrasekhar are the living examples. Personal experience of the cure of seven incurable diseases has convinced me beyond any doubt.

3] Supraconscious or transcendental level of consciousness which resides in the Universe in the form of God's aura and covers all the planets in all the galaxies. This wonderful all pervasive benevolent healing energy functions on love. Hence the love [sneha] is the most powerful Primary Motivational Factor [PMF] for any living form or being. This cosmic energy is running the affairs of the whole Universe tirelessly and without any glitches for eternal number of years. Modern science has not been successful in creating such inexhaustible source of energy.

HUMAN CONSCIOUSNESS

We shall discuss human consciousness first because the cosmic consciousness remains a debatable entity and meets with several conflicting controversies. All of these are detrimental to individual mental peace and our desire is to have a global peace.

Research in Mind Body Medicine tells us that a human being is a BMSO- Body Mind Soul Organism. Soul has inherent consciousness that manifests as Mind, Intellect and Traits. **Receptorology** tells us that BMSO car is driven by soul and governed by several powerful minute "Points." God, soul, acupuncture and acupressure points and Energy chakras are metaphysical. That means the science in spite of magical advances is ignorant about the existence of **metaphysical** entities. Cerebral genes shown by Allen's brain map, Somatic genes and receptors are a physical reality as proved by medical science.

Body aura surrounding each one of us is due to the incessant vibrations emanating from the soul. The colour of aura due to vibrations from the soul changes according to the type of thoughts and emotions. The vibrations from a soul stabilized in higher plane of Consciousness are responsible for a white, bright and well demarcated aura around an individual. **The tint** of Vikalpa, Vikara, Vasana and Vikshepa **tainting the pure and clear consciousness** displays different hues of colour on Kirlian Body Aura Photography. Medical wing of BK-R.E.R.F. has certain novel instruments which demonstrate aura as well as the transcendental stages of consciousness. Thought graph Machine in BK S.P.A.R.C. wing shows a fish in ocean getting transformed into an angel on achieving deeper meditative states. Portable **Aura scanner Happiness index Machine** of BK Dr. Chandrasekhar and RespErate machine [USA] are useful instruments for deep research on meditation. But these instruments remain to be validated. Secondly, a uniform and **universally accepted**

definition of complex meditation technique is not yet available. I have suggested a composite definition for universal acceptance in my first book entitled "Spiritual Medicine for modern lifestyle diseases". But as per Drama the world of research remains ignorant about such suggestion. **The apathy of the BK- Medical wing and in fact, whole of BK-world is phenomenal and astonishing.**

Dadi Janaki, the international head of Brahma kumaris, has been certified as the most stable mind [Sthit-**pragnya state of consciousness] by two independent teams of neurophysicians in USA and Australia.** Her body aura was tested using a novel Gas Diffusion Visualization technique. Her aura went out beyond the limits of recording plate with deepening stages of meditation.

Bhagavad Gita describes two main types of Human consciousness- 1] Body consciousness and 2] Soul consciousness. The whole spiritual effort [Purusharth] in BK-Rajayoga is aimed at losing deeply entrenched Body consciousness and transforming into the highest, purest and most powerful **Brahma Baba Type of consciousness.** This stage is a precursor to stabilizing the soul perpetually into higher **deity like consciousness**.

HUMAN CONSCIOUSNESS AND CHARAK SANHITA

One thousand years old Charak sanhita describes 15 types of personalities [Prakruti] based on the types of consciousness. Thus this treatise is the foundation to understanding the Whole Person Medicine that is the current craze in USA. Several Rejuvenation clinics have mushroomed in USA and making thriving business by administering nothing more than a fragrant soap enema. Non-vegetarian diet gives a sordid constipation. All of the accumulated toxins and waste material comes out making the person feel very light, energetic and happy. Ancient **Kaya kalpa** by Ayurvedic chikitsa [Therapy] by herbs gave permanent rejuvenation and youthfulness. But the valuable knowledge about the herbs has been lost to the posterity. Several Ayurvedic chikitsalaya in South of India are now competing with "Enema Clinics" and trying very hard to turn the persons with most corrupt psyche into ageless Yayatee, father of Bhishmacharya. He made his son to vow that he shall never marry and be a competitor to his progeny from new found youth. In return he gave his son the power of **Ichchamaran** [power to leave the mortal coil at one's own will].All of this mythology is simply mind boggling for a scientist mind. But one lesson that the story of

Bhishmacharya taught me is not to take any kind of vow. This foolish vow has made the immortal Bhishmacharya to remain on the side of **Adharm. Brave and very powerful Rajaputs** have been the great sufferers of wisdom less vows. "Prana jayee par vachan na jayee is foolish vow" for it hands over the remote of your decision into unsavoury hands. Beautiful and brave Jodhabai had to marry a Muslim king Akbar. Powerful Rajput army fought against Maharana Pratapsinh. Whole of Ramayana occurred only because Maharaja Dashrath handed over the remote of his decision into the hands of Maharani Kaikeyee. This wisdom less maharani listened to the bad advice of crooked Manthara.

Charak classifies Human consciousness into three main types-

1] Satvik
2] Rajasik
3] Tamasik.

Highest level of **Satvik consciousness** is known as Brahma type. **Rajasik consciousness** desires to enjoy what this limited life has to offer. It easily succumbs to temptations, attractions and sensual and sexual pleasures. This consciousness is always in search of new openings for enjoyment. LGBT is the propensity by this type of consciousness. Health and wealth eventually gets lost and the life becomes a hell due to pain, suffering and financial miseries. This consciousness is frequent victim of Devil in the form of "Honey trap" and "Money trap." High Achiever Syndrome is frequent and fashionable manifestation. The person wants to achieve more and more by any means. Politicians are class apart in this category. Today doctors in the healing profession also form a long queue.

Tamasik is the most basal level of consciousness with feeble intellect, vicious temperament and an insatiable love for the pleasures of food and those of flesh. Laziness, lack of alertness, lack of attention and limited grasp of intellect are the hall marks.

Scientist Mind in dominant hemisphere of brain is the seat of Rajasik and Tamasik consciousness. Hence whole of spiritual effort is directed towards silencing this naughty mind to achieve Antar mauna. The **inner giant** called as Spiritualist Mind then awakens to its full potential. This mind always harbours soul consciousness. Perpetual spiritual effort raises this consciousness to higher and higher levels until stabilization in a deity like pure consciousness is achieved. This state is known as stage of spiritual equilibrium or **Sthit-pragnya avastha**.

STHIT-PRAGNYA AVASTHA OF CONSCIOUSNESS

The person, whose consciousness is stabilized in the state of spiritual equilibrium similar to that of **Brahma Baba,** automatically acquires certain unique capacities and powers:-

1] Mindfulness-
The person has a power to establish his mind firmly on any given positive thought [Sankalpa] at any moment for any length of time. The mind is totally focussed **[Ekagra chitta avastha]**. as well as relaxed and happy[**Sat-chitta-anand avastha**].Body became totally relaxed[**Shavasan**]. Dr. Herbert Benson, American cardiologist and the founder of the first institute of Mind Body Medicine in 1970 called Ekagra chitta avastha as **The zone** and Shavasan as Biological Relaxation Response **[BRR]. Therapeutic importance** of these two states is that autosuggestions and visualization become very effective bringing a radical transformation of Nature[Vrutti].Impossible cures happen because the release of rejuvenating neuro-hormones- Encephalin, Endorphin, Anandamide, Melatonin, BDNF- Brain Derived Neurotropic Factor, Sirtuins, Receptor Modulation Factor and Stem Cell Activation Factor. This pharmacopoeia of

God brings about impossible cures by restoration of **internal balance.**

2] Cosmic Healing Vibrational Whisper-
Dr. Naras Bhat, Professor of Mind Body Medicine at Seybrook University, USA, in his book – "Reversing Heart attacks, cancer and ageing", describes a cosmic healing vibrational whisper that traverses through the seven energy chakras during the state of Transcendence and brings about healing and rejuvenation. The practitioner may have an "Experience" of an energy [Chaitanya] created in whole of his body. No wonder BK-Rajayoga calls the meditative experience as **"Battery charging."** He also informs that a single thought if repeated several times daily in the states of "BRR and the Zone" for 21 days then the person manifests the qualities [**Swaroop Banana**] that have been repeated in such autosuggestion and visualization.

3] Internal Silence [Antar mauna]-
Turbulent Scientist Mind is totally silenced and the powerful Spiritualist Mind takes over the matters in its hands. Intuition or gut feeling is enhanced giving forewarnings about an impending peril or about the harmful intentions of other human being. An out of box thinking or Lateran thinking gives innovative and effective solutions to the problems at hand. Two seconds snap judgements about the

other individual come out to be the best and most effective. **Malcolm Gladwell** describes in book "Blink", a "Harding error" which negates this power of accurate judgment about the other person. The famous "**Body consciousness**" attracts the mind to the external beauty of the person and ill judgement happens. Beautiful ladies as spy always manage to create a "**Harding error**" in the judgement by the excellent spies. James Bond appears to be an exception. His chosen lady always seems to be a correct choice.

4] Losing Body consciousness-
Celestial Muralis of Shiv, the Supreme soul, prescribe one **genie like exercise** for losing Body consciousness. The power of mindfulness is highly beneficial in this exercise.

BK spiritual concepts tell that soul or Atman manifests three different morphological forms- Sakari [corporeal], Akari and Nirkari [incorporeal forms]. Soul in our body is known as Sakari form. Soul coming out of mortal coil and acquiring a micro-body of orange red colour is known as Akari or Farishta form.

During Amrit vela meditation[4am meditation] one has to do this genie like exercise until one could assume any form in a fraction of a second automatically and easily.

5] Safeguard against criminal eye-

The person develops a miraculous power of "Not seeing even when he is seeing." This helps him to safeguard himself from short provocative clothes, nudity and other forms of provocation. The research by Dr. Vikram Lele, Director of Radiology and PECT at Jaslok Hospital, Mumbai in the year 1987 at Germany using advance PECT procedure gives the explanation for the development of such unique power in a BK- meditator. His study showed hypo metabolism in certain posterior region of the brain involved in vision. Thus the person is able to prevent the sensory input for seeing at his will. This helps a BK-practitioner to obey the command by Shiv Param-Atma to safeguard oneself from developing criminal eye. Our eyes form the window through which the **kaam -Vika**ra [Lust] enters our consciousness.

6] Metta Bhavana –

Metta Bhavana is a Buddhist concept and a stage in Vipassana which involves wishing well for each and everybody in the world. This shubh Bhavana, Shubh kamana and shubh chintan should encompass even those whom you perceive as your enemy. Brahma like consciousness does not have an enmity, jealousy or hatred for anybody and perceives each other person as a soul, and a roohani or spiritual brother. In this way the Shubh chintan becomes easy and automatic.

7] Seva or Service to other human beings-

Seva is one of the pillars of BK-Rajayoga along with simaran or Yaad [remembrance]. One could do seva in three ways- By words [**Vacha**], by acts [**Karmana**] and through Mind [**Manasa**]. All types of seva require stabilizing the consciousness on higher planes [Yog-yukta]. Then one has to be selective [Raj-yukta] evaluating the level of other person's grasp and understanding. Finally one has to use his skills of diplomacy [Yukti-yukta] so that one does not offend the existing beliefs and the faith of other person. Brahma type does seva by using all of these propensities.

Pure and powerful personality [Purushottam] emanates the most powerful and pious vibrations. Faraday cage experiment proves that thought vibrations could travel to an infinite distance. Thus Brahma type consciousness could send vibrations of peace, power and purity to the souls of the whole world.

Brahma Kumaris is a global NGO which has consultative status in UNO. It has won six global peace awards. It is believed that the unending Vietnam war stopped because of the group meditation by Brahma Kumaris for global peace.

BK Dr. Chandrasekhar using his aura scanner has shown that my aura reached up to a magical 135 feet. Normal range is 10-12 feet. Dr. Naras Bhat in USA used RespErate and discovered that my respiration came down to just two per minute after a brief meditation. Normal range is 16-18 per minute. Scientist of S.P.A.R.C. wing at Mount Abu using Thought graph machine, found that a brief mediation takes me to the deepest level and announces that I have become an angel. But my Scientist Mind is raising a question- **"How one could rely on the results using the instruments which have not been validated?"** So right now my telling about such results amount to a quackery and practicing **Pseudoscience.**

8] Cosmic travel in angelic form [Farishta swaroop]-

One of the Muralis by incorporeal Shiva gave unbelievable information. Elevated souls shall move all over the world emanating vibrations of peace, purity and power in their angelic form [Akari avastha] as part of seva for global welfare [Vishwa Kalyan]. The people on earth shall wonder at such UFOs –Unidentified Flying Objects. Scientists in NASA shall investigate and tell that UFOs are the Flying vehicles used by aliens with far superior brains. When you come back to earth after doing Seva, everybody shall realize that UFOs are the angelic forms of Brahma Kumars.

My Scientist Mind simply refused to believe. But my "Experience" of last 21 years has shown me that it is foolish to believe that an entity does not exist simply because it is beyond the limited grasp of a human being. Para normal world and ghosts do exist. Doctors refuse to believe in Sakashtkars [Mystical experiences] as hallucinations [Bhrum] also occurs in the same area of brain. The famous Chillum, the hall mark of some of the saints gives strength to their wrong belief that spiritual knowledge **[Gyan]** is the product of hallucinations. Both Holy Quran and BK-spiritual concepts owe their existence to mystical experiences. Spiritual knowledge is the conglomeration of knowledge derived from "Experiences" and "Mystical experiences" of highly evolved and enlightened souls. One thousand years old **Mahaavatar Nagraj Babaji** or Kriya Babaji exists even today in Himalayas in the body of 16 years old. Marshall Govindan in his book on Kriya yog tells that Babaji has acquired **Souraba Samadhi**. That means he has achieved conquest over death. Is existing for a definite purpose and he personally guides a sadhak after a certain level of spiritual evolution is attained. He Is it true? God only knows.

There is a slender difference between knowledge, belief, faith and truth. A priest was giving a sermon on the very topic. A person named John got up and started giving a piece of his mind. Wise priest then calmly asked him- "How many children he has?" Mr John answered – "One son". Priest then proceeded to elaborate in a loud voice- "Mr. John has one son. It is the **knowledge** for all of us. Mr John **believes** that master John is his son because he has **faith** in Mrs John. But the **truth** is known only to Mrs John and God."

Chapter-4

Universal Mind, Remote Sensing, Premonition, Remote Viewing, Secret Of Simultaneous Discoveries, Human Mass Excitability Index And Mass Mind Intention

Recent developments in Neuroscience provide scientific evidence for the amazing free of cost knowledge one derives from Foundation course at any of the 11500 BK-Centres in 140 countries; and from Muralis.

Daily Amrit-vela meditation involves contemplation over a single positive thought [Sankalpa].The whole technique of meditation is based on repeated auto-suggestions with single thought of transformation of a particular deficiency in own self and visualization to imagine that a particular Divine quality or power has become part of the psyche.[**Swaroop banana**].Neuroscience **tells us** that a thought if repeated often and daily for 21 days becomes deeply embedded in our psyche and becomes a part of our Nature[Vrutti]. **Sage Patanjali's kriya yog** calls this technique as **Vrutti nirodh.**

Concept of Universal Mind postulates that all pervasive benevolent cosmic consciousness or God's aura forms a cosmic Google and a store house of all the thoughts of all the human beings. In Golden and Silver eras, cosmic consciousness is serene and without any turbulence. So the life is heavenly without any pain, suffering and calamities. But in Iron Age, Human Mass Excitability Index has risen phenomenally. As a result serene lake of Universal consciousness is disturbed and turbulent because of the violent tsunamis of Vikara, Vikalpa, Vasana and Vikshepa in human minds.

Tsunamis of Vikalpa, Vikara, Vasana and Vikshepa in cosmic consciousness start happening from Copper age and become vastly destructive in Iron Age. "Pleasure drugs and abnormal passions," mass killing of dolphins for mere pleasure of killing or mass killing of Buffalos for wrong religious beliefs in Nepal, mass shooting in schools killing several hundreds of innocent children and killing of different animals for palatal pleasure create tsunami of violence in Universal Mind. Powerful Nature then reacts in so many different violent ways. Floods, famine, cloud bursts, earthquakes, bomb blasts, and horrible accidents happen all of a sudden. This cosmic situation has increased **Human Mass Excitability Index**

phenomenally. Anger has become road rage and lust has become violent rape. Terrorism and killing of innocents have become a global affair. Praying in churches has become invitation for bomb blasts. Amassing the Weapons of mass destruction has become a craze. The talks of global peace become ornamental in such situation.

REMOTE SENSING AND REMOTE VIEWING

Some individuals have been endowed with the power of Extra Sensory Perception [ESP]. Such persons could see an event in remote future happening in front of theirs eyes. Impending murder, rape or catastrophe becomes known to them in advance. This power is a curse as correction of the destiny remains beyond their power. THEIR LIFE BECOMES A HELL. This phenomenon is variously labelled as premonition, remote viewing or remote sensing.

PROOFS FOR THE EXISTENCE OF UNIVERSAL MIND

1] Phenomenon of simultaneous discoveries- Several scientific discoveries have happened in a mysterious fashion. Elusive structure of Benzene ring revealed in a lucid dream. Alexander Fleming discovered antibiotic Penicillin by lack of growth of virulent staphylococcal colonies around a contaminant fungal colony on the culture plate. In 1960, Medawar in London and Burnett is Australia independently discovered T and B cell subset population and brought an epoch making change in nascent branch of Immunology. Before 1960, a Lymphocyte was considered as a phlegmatic spectator gathering at the periphery of inflammatory focus for watching the life and death battle between invading Bactria and defending polymorphs. The discovery transformed Lymphocyte into a clever Brigadier using its armamentarium dexterously. Colony Stimulating Factor [CSF] brought about an increase in the strength of defending army. Macrophage Activation Factor made the macrophage more powerful in phagocytosis and destruction of invading bacteria. Complement mediated lysis and several other magical defence mechanisms became known to man. This Raphael in body has been made ineffective by the opposition by stress hormones.

2] Bhrugu sanhita –

This ancient Indian scripture has the record of each life and death of every individual on the planet earth. That means the BK-concept of fixed and limited number of souls in Param-dham [Supreme abode of all the souls] is absolutely correct. Each soul after death is allotted a specific slot according to its karma. Some souls with deity like consciousness are dispatched to Earth to play their role in the world drama from the beginning of eternal time cycle. The souls taking birth in Copper age and Iron age are categorized in specific slots and appear on earth at specific pre-ordained times.

3] Magical Tamra patal and Swarna patal-
The incidence elucidating the existence of these magical patals or screens has happened in my life. My cousin, Mr Shyam Karanje in Mudebidre was frantically searching for me. Both of us did not know about each other's existence. The reason for the search was also mind boggling. My cousin was having a consistent dream in which Shiv Param-Atma was repeatedly requesting him to restart pooja ceremonies in our ancestral temple. He was willing to do it of his own. But the priest told **him** that first he has to perform Vaakk-shuddhi pooja along with the other line of heritage. Question was put in Swarna patal and the answer eventually led to finding me in Mumbai. Vaakk-shuddhi pooja was necessary as our ancestors fought with each other and my forefathers came to Mumbai.

I now believe that science may not able to prove or give logical and scientific explanation. But that does not mean that such inexplicable mysteries do not exist.

MASS MIND INTENTION

BK-Spiritual concepts as told by Shiv, The Supreme Soul, include one wonderful technique to counteract against violent turbulence in Universal Mind called as **Manasa Seva.** This technique of sending the thought vibrations of peace to all the souls in the world is very helpful for participating in Shiva's **Vishwa Kalyan yagnya.** Service through thought vibrations is very scientific as evidenced by following findings-

1] Faraday cage experiment –
Russians used this experiment for espionage. Powerful thought transmitters and sensitive thought receivers were identified by methods known to Russians. Faraday cage is a sealed room which did not allow anything to get in or to get out. Thought transmitter was seated inside the cage. Thought receiver was seated outside the cage. But he was moved away from the cage in a graded fashion. Both were provided a log book. Thought transmitter recorded the time and the thought that was dispatched. Thought receiver recorded the time and thought that was received. The experiment revealed that the thought vibrations could travel to an infinite distance. Thus the claim that a third degree Reiki master sitting in India

could really cure a person in London; is not a myth but reality.

BK-Rajayoga advises to do Manasa seva at Amritvela [4am to 5am] as during this time a majority in the whole world is sleeping and there is no impendence of their thought vibrations. **A sadhak then transmits the vibrations of peace, power and purity to the whole world.**

2] Power of group meditation-
Journal of offenders and rehabilitation records a finding about groups of meditators. They used to gather on a specific day and at specific time every week. Very soon the crime rate of Washington DC came down to a phenomenal 72 per cent. That means the Human Mass Excitability Index somehow came down magically by group meditation. These weekly meetings stopped after few years. Within a short time the crime rate rose rapidly to the original level. It is believed that the unending Vietnam war came to an end because of the group meditation by Brahma Kumaris organization.

3] Dr. Hew Len's Ho'oponopono- Heal thyself to heal the world-
Hawaiian spiritual practice of Ho'oponopono involves wishing good for everybody [Shubh **chintan**]. Dr. Hew Len, Hawaiian psychiatrists

used this technique to increase health and happiness in psychiatry ward he managed. The ward lodged criminally insane and highly dangerous patients. Psychiatrists quit on a monthly basis. The staff frequently called in sick or quit. People would walk through the ward with their backs against the wall, afraid of attack from the patients. Dr. Len started a novel experiment with Ho'oponopono. Dr. Len took patients' case files to his chamber after the ward round and reviewed each case individually. He took on the pains and problems of his patients as if they were his own. Then he worked on healing the issues within himself. His Ho'oponopono consisted of holding each patient's case paper in hand for some time and repeatedly saying- "I love you. I am sorry. Please forgive me." Within few months of this novel practice a miracle happened. Patients who were shackled were allowed to walk freely. Others who were heavily medicated started getting off their medication. The persons who had absolutely no chance of getting out were released. Staff began to enjoy coming to work. Absenteeism and turn over disappeared. Soon the staff outnumbered the patients. Today, that ward is closed.

Whole mind boggling episode raises some very curious questions-

How wishing well and talking to bed tickets resolved the problem? Is it because benevolent thought vibrations reached each particular patient? Is it only thought vibrations that have healed the patients? How thought vibrations could heal an abnormal psyche? Do they activate inherent pranik healing mechanisms in an individual and bring about a release of rejuvenating healing neurohormones from brain?

ENERGY DRIVEN EVOLUTION

Recently it was discovered that Dolphin genome and human genome are basically same. Few chromosomal rearrangements changed how the genetic material was put together. It is concluded that DNA is a wave structure that could be rearranged.

There are several live forms that could re-write their own genetic code. Oldest example is Trypanosoma brucei giving African sleeping sickness. This organism rapidly rearranges its own DNA. As a result it becomes immune defence mechanisms of the host. Immortal jelly fish could completely rewrite its own DNA in the presence of starvation. As a result muscle cells could become nerve cells or even sperm or eggs. Stem cells in human beings are totipotent. That means they could transform themselves into cartilage in knee, heart muscle in damaged myocardium or liver cells in damaged liver.

Lazarus effect- shows that an animal species could spontaneously reappear after millions of years of extinction.

It has been shown that if two persons live in close proximity for long periods of time, 25 years or more, a spontaneous genetic transfer occurs and they develop similar facial features.

Gariaev experiment-
Dr. Gariaev sent a non-burning green laser beam through salamander eggs and then reflected the beam into frog eggs. Amazingly salamanders hatched from the frog's genetic material.

Mass Human Evolution-
It has been scientifically proved that Mass Human Evolution is energetically directed and it has been speeding up for last forty thousand years. This is the result of n active working presence which David Wilcock calls as the Source Field. **Alchemy of God,** a group of brilliant BK-scientists call this Source Field as God's energy aura.

Flynn effect-

Flynn, a New Zealand scientist discovered that approximately 1800 genes or 7 per cent of all human genetics has undergone spontaneous mutation giving an indication of emergence of a higher, stronger and highly intelligent human race. **Is it the indication that the Golden era is round the corner? IQ scores are consistently going up.** Psychologists have changed the scoring system. Shockingly the persons who scored best 10 per cent a hundred years ago would now be in weakest 5 per cent.

The Backster effect-

Backster was working for CIA-Central Intelligence Agency and worked with truth serum and polygraphs. Backster's secretary purchased a rubber plant and gifted it to Backster. One night he connected this rubber plant to polygraph machine. The machine surprisingly recorded a tracing similar to reaction pattern in human beings. So Backster dipped one of the leaves in hot coffee. Nothing happened. He tapped the leaves with his pen. There was hardly any response. Then while packing up for the night he had a thought while washing hands quite a distance away from the plant-"I would get a match and burn the plant's electrode leaf. The very moment the imagery of burning that leaf entered Backster's mind, polygraph recording pen moved rapidly to the top of the chart, a panic reaction.. It was as if the plant has read Backster's mind. Then Backster removed the threat by returning the matches to secretary's desk. Eventually after some time the tracing returned to original calmness.

Amazing Italian scientist Pier Luigi Ighina-
Ighina, a student of Marconi inventor of radio, prepared several devices which replicated the magical effects of pyramidal energy. **Elios device** purified foods after zapping them. Another device called **Stroboscope**. It could create a growing hole opening up in the clouds within a matter of minutes. Ighina discovered that the atoms do not oscillate but vibrate. The vibrations could be changed by magnetic field oscillator like stroboscope. On one occasion he set his apparatus before an apricot tree He then altered the atomic vibrations to that of an apple tree. Within 16 days **apricots mutated into apples** Thus transfer of genetic material is possible without any genes operating. Ighina was able to transform the tail of a rat to that of a cat. Ighina postulated that **cancers could be cured** by gradual alteration in their vibrational index. Adaptive mutation is the hidden law of Nature.

Popp's discovery, Genetic reconstruction and healing —

Popp found that fleas, fish and other organisms are all absorbing light [photons] from each other. He also found out that under stress, we release lot light energy [photons] that is stored in our DNA.
Popp then tested a variety of plant extracts to see if any one of them could actually change the quality of light emission from human body with a view to find out cure for the light-scrambling effect of the cancer cells. But unfortunately everey substance made the problem worse.

Dr. Lew Childre's and Dr. Rein's experiments revealed that he was able to wind or rewind DNA STRANDS in the laboratory from thousands of miles away by focussed thought. Secret lied in generating the coherence in their brain wave pattern. Dr. Rein proved that love **[sneha]** has direct measurable effect on DNA. Love has now been proved as the **basic principle of universal or cosmic energy.**

Dr. Kaznacheyev started with two hermetically sealed cell cultures and infected one of them with a virus. When he shone the light from the diseased cell culture into the healthy cell culture, the healthy cells mysteriously got infected with the disease. The only way this could have happened is if the

DNA inside the healthy cells actually rearranged to form viral DNA. The virus then cannibalized the cellular material of the healthy cells to form more virus.

Dr. Peter Gariaev collected seeds that have died from radiation from the Chernobyl nuclear disaster. Amazingly, by simply shining a non-burning healing green laser light through healthy seeds of the same variety and redirecting that light into dead seeds, the radiated cells miraculously recovered. They were completely healed. They could grow into fully healthy adult plants. Dr. Gariaev tried similar experiment on lab rats. He gave them alloxan to destroy pancreas and produce alloxan Diabetes. The rats died within six days. Gariaev removed the pancreas from a healthy rat, shined a laser beam through it and redirected the light into a rat that was poisoned with Alloxan. These healing results were similar to those found with pyramid energy. He postulated that a "Specific Energy signature" exists in DNA which could be responsible for such miraculous healing. But unfortunately Bauman's State University in Moscow declared it as "**Pseudoscience.**

Psychic Energy vampires-
Dr. Burlakov put growing fish eggs next to each other so that light could pass between them even

though they were hermetically sealed. He discovered to his amazement that if he put older more mature eggs in front of younger eggs, the older eggs sucked the life force out of the younger eggs. This could explain why all of us experience an **"Energy drain,"** in the company of certain individuals. So the concept of psychic vampires is not a myth but a reality.

Spiritual Healing-
Dr. Daniel Be nor analysed 191 cases of spiritual healing. Amazingly 64 per cent showed statistically significant healing effects. In several cases the healing was performed over substantial distance. This study provides scientific proof for **Reiki healing from a great distance.**

About 36 per cent of these studies did not show any healing effect. Mainstream medicine and modern medicine focus only on the experiments that failed and promptly apply a label of **"Pseudoscience"** to all such studies. A spiritual Guru like Ramdeo baba and all the persons in Health care profession are working for achieving only one goal- "Health for all at reasonable price." The patient is bothered only about relief from diseases, pain and suffering. **But in Kali yug Ramdeo Baba becomes a laughing stock in medical profession and the mainstream medicine** that is propelled by abnormal greed receives all the respect in the society.

Dr. Alexandra David Neel visited Tibet in 1920. Her stunning observations appear in a classic in 1931 entitled "With mystics and Magicians in Tibet." Tibetan monks explained to her that all of their mystical abilities came from being able to harness waves of thought energy [**Sankalpa Shakti**] through meditation.

The Secret Of Psychic Training Consists In Development Of Power Of Concentration Of Mind greatly surprising even the abilities of great men with great achievements. The spiritual practice makes the thoughts more coherent and increases the capability to connect with **cosmic consciousness easily and automatically.** This increase in coherence has brought down the crime rate down to phenomenal 72 per cent by th group of meditators in Washington DC.

LUNG- GOM-
Spiritual powers generate enough coherence so that one could levitate own body. Tibetan monks are able to go in deep stance state and **in this state of consciousness** they could run along in huge leaps at remarkably fast speeds using their bodies in a way that completely defies gravity. The monks use this Lung-gom to travel vast distances rapidly.

Each leap may lead them to travel thirty feet high and hundred feet forward. Dr. Alexandra David Neel had witnessed this amazing feat. It believed that the youngest Lama who has come to India in a mysterious way had used this technique.

Dr. Claude Swanson described one Peter Sugleris who had the power of telekinesis and **levitation**. He could bend spoons or move objects merely by looking at them. In 1986, his wife photographed him as he hovered eighteen inches of the kitchen floor and stayed there for forty seconds. The exertion exhausted him and it took some 15 minutes to come back to normal consciousness.
There are several well documented case of human levitation by Christian saints and yogis.

RELEVANCE OF SCIENTIFIC OBSERVATIONS TO SPIRITUAL HEALING BY BK- RAJAYOGA

BK-Rajayoga spiritual practice involves Amrit vela Yaad for attaining purest and the highest state of consciousness [Deity-like], regular attendance for Murali at the BK-centre and Manasa seva. All of these are essential ingredients for spiritual evolution and all of them have a scientific base.

1] Amrit vela Yaad-

The aim is to obtain a single pointed laser beam **focus** of positive thoughts [Sankalpa].The resultant Zone and Biological Relaxation Response gives the miracle of Cosmic Healing Vibrational Whisper traversing through the seven energy chakra and distributing the Life Force Energy to various organs and tissues. Greater Right and left brain coherence is observed in brain wave pattern due to the Zone or Ekagra Chitta avastha. In short a rejuvenation as well as purification of consciousness happens. The release of rejuvenating neurohormones also happens concomitantly.

2] MURALI AND SANGH YOG [Group Meditation]-

Psychic energy vampires prove that psychic energy transfer is a reality. The participants in Sangh Yog are connected to Supreme Powerhouse through meditation. So the question of any soul suffering from "Energy depletion" never arises. At the same time Nature tries to equalize all the souls in terms of energy by passive transfer of life force energy from more powerful souls to less powerful souls. Thus everybody in the group gets empowered.

3] **Energy driven evolution and adaptive mutation of the genes and cure of the diseases-**

Coherent laser beam thoughts during meditation could be analogous to healing green laser beam. The laser has light energy waves and positive thoughts have thought- energy waves. In this way the thought energy waves could have a power to modify the bad genes of Diabetes, Heart attacks or cancer. So it is possible that volcanic Rajayoga meditation could give impossible cures like **EcaP** – Exceptional Cancer patients who became completely cancer free in Bernie Siegel series by Mindfulness programme.

A systematic multi-centric research on meditation appears to be necessary.

Chapter-5

Receptorology And Disease Less And Infection Less World

PREAMBLE-
Shiv the Supreme Soul in His Divine Muralis tells that "Vidhi se hi siddhi hai. Follow the technique meticulously and you shall acquire super human powers [**Siddhis**]."

I have been doing diligent Rajayoga in accordance with **Shrimat** [Divine dictates in Murali] for last 21 years since my **initiation into Rajayoga** at the Meditation Hut and Peace Park situated in the divine campus of Sir J J Hospital, Mumbai. This campus is celestial. It owes its existence to the exceptional philanthropy of one divine soul- **Sir Jamashetji Jeejeebhoy** who donated his entire life's earnings for making this hospital a reality. The medical students in this divine hospital undergo holistic development. Hence like **Dr. Jairam**, the Dean of Bombay Hospital and Padmashree **Dr. Shashank Joshi** [Director of Endocrinology division at Lilavati hospital] and **Dr. Pannikar** [Internationally renowned Diabetologist] become living examples of successful clinicians and administrators. The famous war cry of Gmsites- **"Chuk ruk chuk ruk chuk chuk chuk"** attracts a Gmsite to you anywhere in the world.

Last 21 years of my life I am experiencing as if the Omnipotent God, my Supreme Father, Supreme Teacher and Supreme Sadagati data is by the side of me taking care of all problems and adversities. I had the "Experience of most troublesome **"Double Saade saati"** [Victim of anger of Shani dev or Saturn.]for 15 years while working at Swami Ramanand Teerth Rural Medical college at Ambejogai, Maharashtra as Professor. I was ignorant about Shiv Param-Atma and His Rajayoga. So I suffered maximally. Super human stress in these years gave seven incurable stress associated diseases including Thyrotoxicosis to me. **Practice of Rajayoga** gave emancipation from all the physical diseases as well as **dis-eases of the mind or soul** like stress, tension, anxiety, worry, fear and frustration. But recently I accidently discovered that my current **Saade saati has ended without even realizing that it existed.** My brother-in-law, who is a Scorpio, faced gruesome problems during the current phase of anger by Saturn. This was the personal experience of **Mahavakya** in Murali- "Suli par chadhana thaa, kante par nibh jayega, aur kanta lagana thaa, wo bhi nahi lagega"

Very recently on Ram navami last year in 2018, I came to realize how seriously and sincerely Shiva the God, fulfils His guarantees. My elder daughter, a Dentist, my son in law, and grandson were going to Ganapati Pule. On way on Mumbai Goa road they had head on collision with a truck. The brand new car was a total wreck. But modern safeguards like air bags came immediately to rescue. Both my daughter and son in law on front seats suffered only from a temporary shock. Grandson on back seat fell down and was having a nose bleed. We doctors perceive nose bleeding as myriads of complications. Two Muslim gentleman in following car came and helped my daughter and son in law to get out. Smoke was coming. So they immediately disconnected the battery terminals and then very gently took my grandson out. They directed to collect mobile, purse and all the valuables. They also assured that they are from the nearby village .So they guarantee that not a single bolt would be stolen from the car. Then they took all of them to a well-equipped and well managed very clean Medical college and Research Institute. Grandson was immediately admitted to ICU. Fortuitously, one of the colleague Professor of Physiology and former Dean of Thane Medical college, had joined this private institute after retirement. Her resident rapidly moved the machinery. All the investigations and check-ups were done very fast. Excellent staying and catering arrangements were done for my daughter and son in law. Next day all specialists declared that all is well.

The most surprising part of whole episode was the Murali of few days ago- Shiv Supreme Soul said" If you just remember me by imagining that you are a conscient point of light and who has connected with me , also a conscient point of light, then I guarantee that I shall move holding an umbrella above you and shall take care of all the calamities."
In short, Murali not only forewarns but also guards completely.

One amrit vela meditation I got a "Touching" that I should try for **Dr. Hardas-Pathak oration award** with a novel topic which is the title of this chapter. Immediately God's wheel moved into motion. **Dr. Sarala Menon** and **Dr. Chchaya Chande**, both my colleagues at Sir J J Hospital, Mumbai helped me to complete all the formalities with the help of **Dr. Ashok Pathak**, former Dean of Government Medical college , Miraj. As a result I became chosen for the oration award at regional conference at LTMC, Sion. The topic generated a lot of curiosity in medical circles. Many commented that it seems I am after closing their healthcare business. I told them that **healthcare** is never expensive. It is the

five star sickness care industry that is far beyond the reach of a common man.

Take home message is that Supreme soul Shiva's Rajayoga is a free of cost panacea for all the ills of modern life.

The contemplation in the amrit vela meditation brought forth a novel idea about the various "Powerful Points" that control the functioning of the super duper car, **BMSO-Body Mind Soul Organism**, or a human being, created by Supreme Creator.

A short list of these **"Points"** is as under-
God, soul, Energy chakras, acupressure and acupuncture points, cerebral genes revealed by Allen's brain map, somatic gene and receptors.
Receptor is an omnipotent and omnipresent **point** in human body. It is like zero which indicates both the beginning and end of both positivity and negativity. In short, sky is the limit for its potential. In this light, I perceived BK-Spiritual Knowledge as **"Bindoo shatra** or Science of Points". **Receptorology** for this science in spiritual knowledge appeared to satisfy my hidden desire of dabbling in medical jargons.

Receptor is a point where the enzymes, hormones, antibodies, microbial antigens, toxins, bacteria, viruses, fungi, parasites etc require to get attached first and then and only then they could penetrate inside the host cells to give diseases.

Receptor Modulation Factor [RMF] is possibly produced during **mindfulness indicated by the zone[Ekagra chitta avastha] and BRR-Biological Relaxation Response.** This RMF has immense potential to liberate the mankind from pain and sufferings due to infection and stress borne diseases. The receptors get blocked or inactivated or may be that they undergo adaptive mutation. As a consequence, the invaders [all the microbes], enzymes of stress, auto-antibodies and stress hormones are unable to get attached to the cell and they get removed harmlessly by the scavenger system of the body. **Infections** cannot just happen because the essential step of colonization in pathogenicity is prevented. The stress hormones could not elicit their harmful effects and all of the NCDs- **Non-infectious Chronic Diseases** get prevented in one stroke. NCD wing of Directorate of Health Services, Maharashtra, could try this strategy with the help of AYUSH Directorate. **I tried for this outcome since 2010 to have a better tomorrow in the present health scenario. But it just did not happen.**

Cortical centres- Each of our sensations are controlled by different cerebral centres. Sex centre controls sex drive. Hunger centre stimulates hunger through secretion of Leptin. Satiety centre gives satisfaction [trupti] after the intake of food. Most important for a spiritualist to know is the existence of a "Reward centre", "Punishment centre" and "Reverberating circuits." This machinery fitted by God is to ensure that a man always commits "Good karma" and its existence provides scientific proof **for Karma theory**. When one performs a good act, Reward centre gets stimulated and releases "Feel Good Hormones". Simultaneous rejuvenation and repair also happens. That is why Shiva the Supreme tells us that "**Khooshi jaisi khurak nahi**. Happiness is the best tonic and medicine." Reverberating circuits maintain this wonderful effect for a very long time. When a man commits a bad act ruthlessly throttling his "Inner voice", "Punishment centre" gets activated. Release of harmful stress hormones happens which in due course give the punishment in the form of one or more of different types of NCDs. Somebody gets Diabetes. His joy from eating sweets disappears. Otherwise one may get cancer. Milder form of cancer happens if the sin is less severe. Most virulent form attacks him if his bad karma is proportionately grave.

Cerebral genes- Allen's brain map has revealed **recently** a set of cerebral genes which are most dangerous. A happy relaxed state of mind keeps these genes inactive. But a mind full of stress, worry, fear or frustration activates them. A release of very powerful enzymes occurs which activate the bad somatic genes of NCDs, especially those of cancer. Surprisingly there are nearly 200 different **oncogenes** giving different forms of cancer. So there are 200 different ways by which God or our bad karma could punish us.

Somatic genes- Innumerable congenital and familial diseases are associated with absence or mutation in these genes. Thalassemia and sickle cell disease could be few of the examples. One disease called multiple sclerosis giving progressive muscular weakness gives real hell for the patient as well as for the relatives as death is because of inability to take breath due to weakened diaphragmatic muscles.

The discussion about metaphysical points like God, Soul, Energy chakras and acupressure points has been done in detail in my book entitled 'Spiritual medicine for modern lifestyle diseases."

TAKE HOME MESSAGE

BK-Rajayoga is a God given health formula dispensed without any cost in 11500 BK-centres in 140 countries. Watch Peace of Mind TV channel 24x7 to listen to BK Shivani, who has become a global face of Brahma kumaris. But listening to her is just a beginning. One must undergo free of cost teaching and training in one of the nearby BK-centre till the last breath for receiving divine directions in Murali for perpetual spiritual evolution and enlightenment. A quantum jump in the Quality of life is experienced in terms of Energy, enthusiasm and Happiness. [EEH value].Proof of the pudding lies in tastingit yourself.

APPENDIX – I

Total Health Programme [T.H.P.]   Free of Cost
Spiritual Health Clinic
Lecture Hall, St. George Hospital, Near C.S.T., Mumbai

AIMS- [BK-COLABA CENTRE]
1. MY SOCIETY, A HAPPY AND HEALTHY SOCIETY.
2. MY HOSPITAL, ADDICTION FREE HOSPITAL

Components of Total Health Programme [09-01-2015]
1. Current Research in Mind Body Medicine - Dr. Dilip V. Kaundinya MD
2. Sukshma Yogabhyas -
3. Pranayama-
4. Scientific BK-Rajayoga- Mindfulness Based Stress Reduction Programme- [R-MBSRP]-
5. Pranayama Motivated Defecation [P.M.D.] – discussed in Appendix-2.

PREAMBLE-
Warning- All type of **asana** and **Shuddhi Kriya** must be performed under the supervision of a **trained yoga teacher** until one gets proficient.

Diet- Yogic Satvik vegetarian food though not mandatory, is helpful in attaining the higher spiritual levels quickly. One must remember that the journey of the spiritual path is long and there are **eight levels of Samadhi in spiritual elevation** and evolution.

Non-vegetarian diet gives shortening of telomeres and early ageing. A homemade Maharashtrian thali is the most balanced diet amongst various choices available. **Padmabhushan Dr. R.D. Lele** has described various **anti-oxidants and immune modulators** in this vegetarian diet in his wonderful book- Ayurveda and modern medicine, published by **Bharatiya Vidya Bhavan, Mumbai, 2001.**

Garlic and onion in food are Tamasik i.e. they generate laziness and sluggishness of mind. Author has experimented and discovered that the Total Relaxation Response of Mind and Body [Biological Relaxation Response, BRR and the Zone, [Ekagra Chitta avastha] is delayed while meditating when such diet or stale food is ingested. Anything that is not prepared freshly or stored in a refrigerator is considered as stale in Yogism.

2.1] It is **customary but not mandatory** to begin Yogic practices by chanting a Mantra.

A] **Sarve sukhinaha santu, Sarve santu niramaya, Sarve bhadrani paschyantu, - maa pasche dukh makpunyat.**

Let all the divine persons be happy and disease free. Even the lowest of animals may be protected for their welfare. If we do not give pain to others, the pain and suffering shall never come our way.

OR

B] Aum chanting - Laghu Omkar and Dirgh Omkar

OR

C] **Gayatri mantra** may be recited for 11 times with **proper phonetics** [vaikhari], Upanshu [mumbling tones or 3] by silently chanting. Gayatri mantra is a **Beej mantra**. That means though a proper phonetics is essential for maximum benefit, a practitioner **may begin chanting in any way**. Over a period of time Divine Grace **[Insha Allah]** gradually brings an improvement to the proper level of pronunciation. Author has experienced this phenomenon. Gayatri Mantra is said to potentiate power of differentiation between right and wrong or Vivek. [Buddhi shuddhak]. **Buddhi or wisdom is different from intelligence.** Intelligence is an ability to learn the skills of livelihood quickly. Wisdom is the ability of the person to use his God given intellect properly in accordance with the **eternal laws of morals and ethics**.

An unpublished study tells that the **basal life force energy [Prana]** that exists in and around us is at the level of **2-3 photons** [Light energy particles]. With regular chanting the energy levels may raise upto 5 photon units. A human being can never progress to seven or eight photon level or the level of **the 8th Sun**. Aditya is the first Sun.

2.2] **Sukshma Yogabhyas** includes training in some simple yogic postures for protecting your neck, shoulder, lower back, knees and ankles and maintaining them in a resilient state throughout life.. Annamaya Kosh is made free of impurities. Deep abdominal breathing technique, a cyber-scan with Heartfelt Resonant imaging [HRI] is done prior to the Kriya.

1] Calana Kriya- Loosening practices:- This Kriya help to improve micro-circulation.
A] Neck bending, rotation and twisting
B] Kati Shakti vikasak [Trunk movement]
C] Knee movements
D] **Simple yogic postures [Yogasana]** which could be done at any age. Thus this Sukshma Yogabhyas becomes useful for Geriatric patients and could be implemented in various Geriatric O.P.D.s

Eg. **Tadasana, Vakrasana, Ardha chakrasana, Trikonasana, Ardhaustrasana,** [in supine posture]:- Pavan muktasana, Sarvangasana, Halasan and Shavasana **[Relaxing posture]**. These yogic postures are performed in prone posture]:- Bhujangasana, Shalabhasana, Naukasana and

Makarasana **[relaxing posture]**. Optional- Uttan tadasana and Vishnu shayyasana

2] **Shuddhi Kriya-** Jala neti, Sinha Mudra, Ashwini Mudra [prevents piles and prolapse of rectum] should be done daily
Jal dhoti should be done daily for one month. Later it should be done on every first day and fifteenth day of each month.
Advanced Yogabhyas includes 1] pada hastasana,2] Bhadrasana3] Ardha matsyendrasana,4] Dhunurasana 5]Matsyasana 6]Pachimotanasana and 7] nauli

2.3] **Pranayama-** Eight types of Pranayama exist. Nadi Shuddhi Pranayama is the simplest. If performed along with Jal Neti and Jal Dhoti is a sure cure for asthma and allergies.
Prana means life or oxygen. Ayama means control. This process ensures **maximization of the use of oxygen** that is inhaled.

A] Anulom-vilom or nadi Shuddhi Pranayam B] Kapalbhati 3] Bhramari 4] Bhasarika, 5] Ujjayi 6] Agnisaar 7] Uddiyan bandha 8] Pranayam proper with fixed durations in set proportions for Rechaka [exhalation], Poorak [inhalation-2, Antar Kumbhak[Holding breath after Poorak]-3 and Rechaka-5. Bahya Kumbhak [optional-10]

Patanjali Kriya

Hath yoga includes all of the above practices and Shuddhi Kriya.

Gyan yoga means Dhyan and Dharana.

Note – Each asana or Kriya should be performed with total focus on the sensations that arise in the body. Every movement should be easy and slow and with a flow. Every feeling should be full of happiness.

DHYAN AND DHARANA

Mindfulness Meditation is the term coined by Dr. Richard Davidson, Professor of Psychiatry, and Wisconsin University, USA. Author has termed BK-Rajayoga as Internal silence [Antar mauna] oriented mindfulness meditation.

BK- Rajayoga- Meditation

It has some similarities with Spiritually augmented Cognitive Behavioral Therapy [S.A.C.B.T.] which is the latest in Psychiatry for mind empowerment.

Brahma Kumaris Rajayoga technique as taught in 11500 BK-centres in 140 countries has the following essential components. Each component augments the beneficial effect of other components. Hence the technique is of paramount importance. *[Vidhi se hi siddhi hai]*. Miraculous benefits are obtained within three months if the technique is followed fully and totally. The schedule should form the total and **indispensible component of daily routine** of a practitioner to derive maximum benefits. This is the much needed lifestyle **modification** today.

Essential Components of BK- Lifestyle

A] **Amrit vela Meditation** at 4am to 5am regularly without break. This period of time is known in scriptures as Brahma muhurtha.

B] Traffic control- A **brief Meditation** for just one minute every one hour. This helps to restore elevated consciousness that is usually lost in the present atmosphere of gross negativity.

C] A brief meditation for ten to fifteen minutes before going to sleep. It wipes out the negative transcription of the mind and ensures a deep and refreshing sleep.

D] News Papers and TV serials give a constant and huge diet of toxic emotions. They should be avoided in the morning and two hours before going to sleep. Toxic emotions and negative thoughts deplete Prana or Life Force Energy. Both of them initiate a subtle onslaught of Free radicals or Terror molecules on Longevity genes. This results in **early ageing**, cataracts and heart attacks.

E] Satvik Paushtik vegetarian food is essential but not compulsory. Food should be prepared and eaten in a happy atmosphere and in remembrance of God. Whole focus [Mindfulness] should be on food and on the act of eating. Thus watching TV serial during eating is strictly prohibited. But for the modern man with TV-addiction this may be difficult. **Mind control by meditation shall help you.**

F] Satsang- Daily visit to a BK centre for listening to Celestial **Murali is considered as the food for the soul or Atman.-**

Murali is a Divine four page script that gives a regular input of **powerfully positive** and motivating thoughts from **Supreme Soul** [Param Atma].The **miraculous mind empowerment** by this simple ritual has to be **personally experienced to be believed. Dr. Naras Bhat ,USA**, in his excellent book entitled Stress Physiology quotes that any positive thought repeated for sizeable duration[may be half an hour or more] for **21 days** is embedded deeply in psyche and brings about a positive behavioral change. No wonder **the figure 21 chosen by Shri Ganesh is very auspicious.**

One can access the Muralis on internet or by watching 24 hours Peace of Mind channel on TV.

TRAFFIC CONTROL
A Brief One Minute Meditation Every One Hour Or So

Bring your consciousness to get focused in the centre of the forehead, in between the two eye brows. This is the site for **Agya Energy Chakra**. This is also the site for the Third eye or a spiritual eye. So Har har Mahadeva means each one of us has a **Third eye**. When it opens in Divine guidance during meditation, all of our negativity gets burnt out.

A single auto suggestion needs to be repeated for the whole one minute-

"I am a peaceful soul. I am a loveful soul, blissful soul, pure soul or powerful soul. I am a soul and I am not this body. I am the metaphysical conscient point of light situated at Agya chakra."

The technique involves visualizing each particular quality of the soul and **dwelling in its "Experience"** for some time. This "Experience" then gets imbibed into your psyche or subconscious mind. This implant of a seed of a thought sprouts automatically when the circumstances require that particular quality. Eg. In an encounter with a troublesome person the qualities of peace, power and compassion get emerged. Soon it has a tranquilizing effect on that troubled soul and the situation is saved. Russian R & D institutes attribute this effect to thought vibrations emanating from the soul of a Sadhak [practitioner].

Human mind is experiential. All of its permanent learning happens by acquiring "Experience." Spiritual knowledge is the conglomerate of "Collective Experiences" and "Mystical experiences [Sakshatkars]" of highly enlightened and evolved souls.

LONG VERSION- RAJAYOGA MINDFULNESS BASED STRESS REDUCTION PROGRAMME [R-M.B.S.R.P.]

MEDITATION DONE AT AMRUT VELA [4am for one hour]

PREAMBLE-

The place fixed for meditation should be the same every day. A pure and powerful atmosphere is created around that place by powerful positive thoughts emanating from Atman during meditation.

Sit comfortably with a straight back on a chair. Sukhasana or Padmasan postures on a mat are the best. This posture keeps the **seven energy** chakras of the body in same alignment. This ensures a free **flow of cosmic energy** through seven energy chakras from the top to bottom- Sahasara, Agya, Vishuddhi, Anahat, Manipura, Swadhishthan and Muladhar chakra. These energy chakras are actually the distribution points [D.P.] for **life-force energy** [Prana]. The flow of cosmic energy is called as Cosmic Vibrational Healing Whisper by Dr. Naras Bhat, a cardiologist and a Mind Body Medicine Specialist in USA. Now perform abdominal type of breathing ten times. This process helps to calm down

R-M.B.S.R.P. involves following techniques:-
A] **Cyber scan** of own thoughts
B] **Heart felt Resonance Imaging [H.R.I.]**- shows the predominant thought or thoughts occupying one's mind and reveals the "Experience" or sensations one's Self or Atman is getting from such thoughts. Vipassana, Buddhist form of Meditation by Lord Gautama Buddha calls this process as "Differential perception." A negative thought or emotion always creates a bad feeling or sensation. Predominant thought forms a Primary Motivational Factor [P.M.F.]for the Atman. Therefore **Bhagavad Gita** tells us that a thought form the seed of our karma and destiny.
C] Auto-suggestions or self-hypnosis
D] Visualization or guided imagery.

E] STEPS OF LONG VERSION MEDITATION
1. Focus
2. Internalization
3. Cosmic Communion.
4. Post Meditation Suggestions [PMS]

First step-   Focus- Bahya Tratak-
Repeat each of the autosuggestions ten times. Visualize whatever words are spoken in the commentary.eg. I am an Ananda swaroop soul. Visualize the moment when you were full of happiness.

A] Give an auto-suggestion number one- I am a soul. **I am not this body.**

I the soul am a metaphysical conscient point of light which is immortal, indestructible and diseaseless. I a conscient of point of light am situated in the centre of the forehead in between two eye brows..

I am a peaceful, loveful, blissful, powerful and **pure** soul.

Purity has three levels-

1] Brahmacharya Celibacy- This is the purity at the level of body consciousness. It is required in **Balya Avastha** or learning phase of life. Our own research [Aurangabad] has proved that chewing five leaves of **Neem** daily helps to achieve celibacy.

Grihasthashram is governed by the rules pertaining to it.

Vanaprastha avastha means a process of withdrawing our consciousness from the external to the internal world. This is an inner **ever blissful voyage** into the fourth dimension- spiritual dimension.

Sanyas- means developing such ruling and controlling power over one's mind that the temptations, attractions and pressures of the external world fail to affect us. This is the state of spiritual equilibrium **[Sthit-pragnya avastha].** Dadi

Janaki , the 100 years old Head of the Brahma kumaris has been certified by neurologists as the most stable mind in the whole world.

2] Purity at the level of thought- Ruling and controlling power over the mind is so powerful that not even one impure thought for any soul arises in the mind.

3] Highest level of purity- when you constantly have only the thoughts about the welfare of all the other persons or animals coming in contact with you. **[Shubh chintan and Shubh chintak]**

Note- A stage may come by the repeated autosuggestions when you shall lose all of the body consciousness and may "Experience" a belief that you a mere conscient point of light. However, achieving this stage requires a very long spiritual effort. But it is also true that till such a **body less state [Ashariri avastha]** is achieved by the consciousness a lifestyle following **Straight Path or Sirat al Mustaqim** takes care of your health, wealth, mental peace and happiness.

B] Now turn your attention to your thoughts.
They usually are running like superfast train in men with very high I.Q. today.
Give autosuggestion for ten times that the speed of thought is getting slower and slower.

C] Now turn your attention to your consciousness-
Perform a detail **Cyberscan** of your thoughts and categorize them into negative and waste thoughts, toxic emotions, positive thoughts and positive emotions. A rough percentage of positive and negative thoughts at this point time shall help to judge your progress and effect of spiritual effort.
Perform **HRI-Heartfelt Resonance Imaging** to decide about the most predominant negative thought/emotion in your mind.
Give autosuggestion-   Let go .Don't get attached to thoughts. The speed of thoughts is gradually reducing.
Now turn your attention to your consciousness [Energy plus awareness].It is scattered like a diffuse sunlight. So it is ineffective.

Give autosuggestion-   My consciousness is getting focused on me, the conscient point of light in the centre of the forehead. Soon a single pointed focused state of consciousness shall be obtained.

As the focus increases the speed of thoughts shall get proportionately reduced. You shall be able to distinguish between the positive, negative and the waste thoughts as well as toxic emotions.[Daniel Goleman]. Desires, Toxic emotions, negative thoughts and waste thought are responsible for the depletion of your pranik strength [Life Force].

Give autosuggestion- All of my desires, toxic emotions, negative thoughts and waste thoughts are getting burnt out in the intense fire of my meditation [Yogagni].All of this negativity of mind is getting permanently deleted from my mind's computer.
A stage shall come when all the negativity shall get deleted from the mind's computer for one particular moment. When this happens, internalization of the consciousness takes place.

SECOND STEP OF R-MBSRP-
Internalization

Internalization of consciousness is indicated by a feeling of totally relaxed states of mind and body with a state of bliss. Dr. Herbert Benson, an American cardiologist who founded the first Institute of Mind and Body Medicine in 1970, uses two terms for denoting these states-
1] Biological Relaxation Response **BRR** [Shavasana] and 2] The zone.**[Ekagra Chitta Avastha]**.

This state of consciousness, a soul conscious or Satvik state is very important.

1] Various autosuggestions become most powerful and effective in this state.

2] Rejuvenating neuro hormones FROM THE BRAIN are secreted in this state.

3] Delta waves of deep sleep pattern are recorded usually after a regular practice [sadhana] of 2 years.

4] Lactic acid giving tiredness is quickly metabolized.

5] Secretion of stress hormones and free radicals stops.

6] Potentiation of immune system happens giving a quantum jump in resistance to infections, cancer cells, allergens and auto-antigens.

7] A quantum Jump in self-determination [Will power], Quality of Life [QOL] and E.E.H. value of life [Energy, Enthusiasm and happiness] happens.

Proof of the pudding lies in tasting it. This is known as "Experiential evidence" which has been in use for tasting the effectiveness of medicinal herbs in Ayurveda. The need for expensive state of art equipment to demonstrate an "Experience" by the practitioner of Yog- Transcendental experience." becomes redundant. One can discover whole of God instead of one God's particle if one has belief and faith.

Medical wing of Brahma kumaris [R.E.R.F.- Rajayoga Education and Research Foundation]has some novel instruments- 1] Thought graph machine [in S.P.A.R.C. wing], 2] Aura scanner 3] Happiness index machine and 4] RespErate . However, these instruments require scientific validation by recognized research institutes.

Some Prototypes of disease-specific autosuggestions

1] Anger management- My anger and irritation has disappeared permanently from my mind's computer. I always remember that I am a peaceful, loveful and blissful soul.

2] Stress management- I am a peaceful, loveful and powerful soul. So the stress, tension, anxiety, worry fear or frustration can never contaminate my Satvik consciousness.

3] R-MBSRT for the prevention and cure of the cancer-

One cancer cell is formed after each 10 raised to 17 cell divisions. Natural Killer cells [NK-cells] are the James Bond of the body. They quickly identify and destroy the cancer cell that has been formed. Hence most of us are cancer free till the last breath. So these autosuggestions may prevent cancer.

Autosuggestion and visualization for prevention and cure of cancer-

A cosmic energy, a cosmic healing Vibrational healing whisper is entering my body through the top most Sahasara energy chakra and passing through all the subsequent energy chakras – Agya, Vishuddhi, Anahat, Manipura, Swadhishthan and Muladhar chakra and bringing a rejuvenation. The fire of meditation is so intense that this cosmic energy is burning out each and every cancer cell in my body. NK-cells in my body are quickly discovering the newly formed cancer cells and destroying them. Thus I am attaining a cancer free state.

4] For De-addiction programme-
All of the addictions happen because of stress after stress, lack of mental peace and happiness in life. So the autosuggestions focus on mental peace and happiness.

Autosuggestion -1- I am a peaceful, loveful and blissful soul. I am so powerful that I can easily resist the urge to drink or smoke for getting a temporary "High".

Autosuggestion-2- The neuro-hormones, DHEA, endorphins and Anandamide are natural and most powerful pain killers and mood elevators. So my feeling of unhappiness is disappearing from my mind. The sense of feeling good is so powerful that I shall never indulge in my addiction which gives only a temporary "High."

5] Performance enhancement-

As the Scientist Mind achieves silence [Antarmauna] lateral thinking or Out Of Box thinking begins. This is responsible for intuition [gut feeling or sixth sense] which enhances the power of split second best decision for the problem solving. The suggestion comes to the mind in a split second as if from cosmos. Creativity of the mind is enhanced which could be of great help in innovation. Artists may create such supreme designs or painting which may appear beyond the scope of human thinking. A man can achieve anything if he has a mind to do it.

Third step of R-MBSRP - Cosmic Communion

Visualization or guided imagery plays a great role in this step.

Visualize that I, the soul, a conscient point of light have come out of my body of five elements and undertaken a cosmic travel to Supreme abode [Param Dham] of all the souls. All of us are mere guests on this planet earth. We descend on the planet earth in the costume or body to play our respective roles in a huge world drama. The costume, the type of life and the role are decided by our past karmic accounts. Good karmic account means happiness, health and harmony. Bad karmic account means diseases, defects, early deaths, accidents, pain and suffering. A human being thus always has two choices in life. Right choice means happy and healthy life.

I am now travelling through the world of stars, moon and the sun. I have now arrived in the Micro-world of the Trinity- Brahma, the Creator and Governor, Vishnu the operator and Mahesh the Destroyer. Mahesh destroys the negativity in my mind. I now enter into Param Dham after taking the blessings from the Trinity.

In Param Dham I am experiencing a joy and peace that is beyond words. I am surrounded by a reddish yellow rejuvenating light. I am now standing in front of God, Shiva, Shiva baba, Who is Supreme Father of all the souls, Supreme teacher and Supreme Sadgatidata data. He is also a Conscient Point of Light and incorporeal. He is a Point in appearance but an ocean of peace, happiness, power and of everything one desires in life. I am His beloved son/daughter. So whatever He has, I have a birth right over it. Red rays of power and white rays of peace and purity are emanating from the Supreme Soul [Param-Atma].I am imbibing theses rays and becoming more powerful and peaceful.

Visualize this scene for quite some time.
Visualize that I am getting richer and richer in eights powers that are necessary in life. The power

of tolerance is most essential. But if while tolerating one gets a constant feeling that only "I" am tolerating and suffering then it is not true tolerance. Cosmic Universal laws tell that acquiring one power attracts other powers as if from Cosmos. Power of judgment and right decision is another very important power of the soul. An "Inner voice" always shouts loudly when a man is about to commit wrong. The right or wrong is decided by eternal cosmic laws. Enhanced power of judgment is necessary for the best solutions to the problems in life. Power of accommodation, co-operation, condensation and power to face and finish are other important powers one acquires in cosmic communion with Supreme Father.

Now I after getting enriched with power and peace I am undertaking the return journey. I have crossed the Micro-world of Trinity and also the world of Sun, Moon and stars. Now I have come to rest on my eternal seat in between the two eye brows.

Visualize- The rays and vibrations of power, peace, purity, love and bliss are spreading through each and every cell of the body rejuvenating and re-charging them. Dwell in this "Experience" for some time.

Post Meditation Suggestions

Now give two auto suggestions to the mind-
1] Let me remain in this elevated powerful soul conscious state throughout the day while performing my tasks under any circumstances which may try to disturb this state of consciousness.
2] Next day, at 4am, Amrit –vela when I begin my meditation [yog with Supreme Soul] let me begin from this elevated state of consciousness so that with each day I shall become more powerful, peaceful, loveful, blissful and pure.

REFERENCES

1. Naras Bhat- Reversing stress and burn out. 2002. Cybernetix Publishing.2182, East Street, Concord, California 94520, USA. Email- StressBook@heartsaver.com

2. Naras Bhat- How to reverse and prevent Heart disease and cancer? 1995. Dr. Kumar Pati at New Editions Publishing1675 Rollins Road, Suit B3,Burlingame, California 94010 phone [415]697-4400 Fax-[415]697-7937

3. Marshall Govindan- Kriya yoga Sutras of Patanjali and the Siddhas. Translation, Commentary and practice. 2000. Babaji's Kriya Yoga Order of Acharyas Trust. Post Box- 5608, Malleshweram West, Bengaluru.560055. email - kriyayog@vsnl.com

4. Satish K. Gupta, Ramesh C. Sawhney, Lajapt Rai, V.D. Chavan, Sameer Dani, Ramesh C. Arora,, V. Selvamurthy, H.K. Chopra,, Navin C. Nanda- Regression of coronary atherosclerosis through healthy lifestyle in coronary artery disease patients- Mount Abu Open Heart Trial. Indian Heart J. 2011;63;461-469

5. S.D. Kaundinya, D.V. Kaundinya: - Meditation versus relaxation- A comprehensive review-International J. of Basic and Applied Physiology. Vol-2,p-240-257;December 2013

6. D.V. Kaundinya – Brahma Kumaris Rajayoga- An evidence based internal silence oriented meditation as cure for the incurable and chronic diseases[NCD] and addictions. International J. of Current Medicine And Applied Sciences. July 2014

APPENDIX – II

Pranayam Motivated Defaecation
A recent survey has shown that 14% of all Indians including the young suffer from mild to severe constipation. Severe constipation is very common in senior age group or the patients in Geriatric O.P.D. Several have to take enema on regular basis. Some have an experience of taking out the faecal nuggets with fingers. Lack of exercise, Pizza Burger Cola diet and Non-vegetarian diet are some of the important contributing factors. Over use of Over The Counter [OTC] pills or purgatives weaken the walls of intestine. Shortly it results in weak peristalsis or propelling movement of the intestine.

Hydrotherapy prior to P.M.D. Programme-
Warning- Never strain while defecating if you wish to avoid piles or fissures. Everything in yogic practices is done with ease.

Prior hydrotherapy- It is necessary to hydrate oneself well one day prior to P.M.D. Drink a minimum of 15 to 20 glasses of water throughout the day. It is necessary to drink water even if one is not thirsty. This is because with advancing age, the reflex initiating the drinking process gets progressively weaker. **The test for adequate**

hydration is that the urine always remains clear like water. Henceforth make it a practice to drink plenty of water throughout your life.

Jal Dhauti is a yogic kriya if performed for one month ensures adequate hydration and effective purging out of accumulated toxins.

Take four to five glasses of water or more if you can, no sooner one gets up at 4am.[Amrit-vela]. Warm water with a pinch of salt is helpful initially. A session of Pranayam after Amrit-vela meditation should be followed by P.M.D. Isabgol at night may help but required only initially. Learning Shuddhi kriyas like Jal Dhauti and Pranayam called Agnisaar helps.

Relaxation of mind by meditation plays a significant role. Never sing – Tu atki hai kanha, main tadapata yanha. This creates a negative programming of your mind. Instead sing. ,"Chal akela chal akela, Tera maila peeche chchuta, tu chal akela. This shall be a positive programming of your mind for the task at hand.

Do not contaminate the elevated Satvik consciousness achieved by meditation by taking a newspaper or your problems to the toilet seat. Focus your attention on your colon. Here the single pointed focus achieved by meditation helps greatly. Visualize about a faecal bolus stuck up at the appendix side of the colon. Now breathing deeply [abdominal breathing] visualize that the bolus is gradually getting unstuck. Now it is moving forward with each progressive contraction of the colon. Agnisaar at this point of time helps. Visualize that the bolus is now travelling in the ascending colon. Now it has entered the Transverse colon. Its forward movement has now become quicker. Visualize that now the bolus has entered descending colon and speedily going to the end of the rectum. Now a final push and it is out of the body. Do not strain at this point of time as it may cause piles to form. Each process has to be done with ease without straining at any point. Immense relief and joy at this point of time is beyond words. In fact you shall also see the relief writ large on the faces of the people around you, especially in an elevator.

Within a month you shall be colon trained and defecation shall be as easy as taking a breath.
BK- Rajayoga restores the SNS Versus PNS balance [Sympathetic Nervous System and Parasympathetic Nervous System] which is usually disturbed in Diabetes. This is the common cause of constipation in Diabetics.

Disturbed Internal balance of ions, sugar and lipids also contribute to N.C.D.s like Head ache,

Migraine, Acidity, High B.P., Diabetes and Heart attacks.

Gut Like Protein –I and II released from Gastro intestinal tract helps in controlling appetite in Diabetes.

Medical science behind each and every ancient yogic practice needs to be investigated by a systematic research in Medical Institutes. There is a paucity of this type of research because the Indians themselves have stopped believing in the ancient Indian spiritual wisdom. Whole of the world is engaged in yog while Indians are pursuing the lifestyle of Bhog and Rog.

09-10-2017
BK Dr. Dilip V. Kaundinya

www.ingramcontent.com/pod-product-compliance
Lightning Source LLC
Chambersburg PA
CBHW031358040426
42444CB00005B/341